LIVE AND WORK IN CANADA

by

Avril Harper

Published by
Grant Dawson, 7 Rockland Road, Putney, London SW15 2LN

LIVE AND WORK IN CANADA
by Avril Harper

Cover Design by
Melmay Design Associates

Other titles in this Series

Live and Work in Central America
(including Mexico and the Caribbean)
Live and Work in the Far East
Live and Work in Germany
Live and Work in Japan
Opportunities Overseas
Worldwide Working Holidays
Travelling the World on a Shoestring
Jobs at Sea

Printed by The Chameleon Press Ltd, 5-25 Burr Road, London SW18 4SG

Contents

The information in this book has been checked as accurate at the time of writing. However, readers should note that details are liable to change without notice. It is essential to recheck before making any commitments or travelling overseas. We strongly advise readers not to travel overseas without taking sufficient funds to support themselves and pay for a return journey home if necessary.

Foreword

The recent break up of the Soviet Union makes Canada now the largest country in the world; a nation thick with snow-encrusted mountains and wide uninhabited wilderness; a land rich in long scenic coastlines where the idle rich and less affluent citizens bare their sun-tanned bodies to temperatures high enough to deter even the most ardent of British sun-worshippers; a land covered in vast areas of farmland and prairie regions parading their natural attributes in much the same ostentatious manner as do the many citadels of silver-clad, glass swamped skyscrapers of Canada's massive multi-ethnic cities.

It's a land where citizens live at one with nature; a land where in many parts it's computers not land that reign supreme. Canada is a land of many contradictions; like a patchwork quilt, one whole but comprising many intricate woven parts; a country rich in widely differing and sometimes unique life styles. Here one might wend one's way slowly through endless motorised crowds in major cities, or else walk or journey otherwise over mile upon mile of wide open prairies and forests in which people rarely detract from that awe-inspiring spectacle of peace and overwhelming solitude.

Life in many ways in very similar to that of the neighbouring United States; yet in just as many ways one might be forgiven for believing that this is a country many thousands of miles removed.

But like any patchwork composition, no individual component can exist in total isolation; none might bear even vague resemblance to those areas to which it is inextricably linked; and yet each needs and depends upon the existence of its neighbour; each contributes towards and compliments the final colourful and multi-faceted spectacle.

This is Canada!

Introduction

Why Live and Work in Canada?

Once that discussion has taken place of the many beautiful parts one encounters in this clean, fresh country; one in which high living standards exist alongside excellent job opportunities, that question will almost certainly be superseded by one of 'Why **not** live and work in Canada?

The almost universally positive answer awaiting the last question might best be illustrated by a survey recently carried out by top United Nations economists, who tell us that for the first time ever Britain has been included amongst the top ten countries in which to live. And what of **Canada**? Number **one** – pushing the seemingly indomitable Japan into second place. Neighbouring United States incidentally weighed in at sixth place.

Canada has a long tradition of attracting British immigrants, in general presenting few difficulties in settling down to a new way of life which many profess is very much reminiscent of their British homeland.

Canadian immigration authorities nevertheless advise that prospective immigrants learn as much about their intended new home before making that vital decision to relocate themselves and their families. And yet Canada presents very little by way of culture shock such as is experienced in various other parts of the world, usually where traditions, culture and living conditions differ widely to those with which one is familiar at home.

Could I Work in Canada?

Canada no longer operates an 'open door' policy in respect of immigrant settlers or foreign workers. As for many other countries her own population suffers heavily under the strains of rising unemployment. Consequently those admitted to work in Canada whether for a short or indeterminate period, must normally offer skills currently in short supply amongst Canadian nationals and landed immigrants. Rigid rules and regulations govern the application of foreign workers seeking employment here, making it illegal to enter the country for the purposes of seeking employment, unless of course permission has first been obtained from immigration officials.

Generally though, it must be said that there are a great many openings for short-term, seasonal and casual work which might be available to the intending working holidaymaker to Canada, many such openings being obtained through such as tourist firms, domestic and au pair agencies, voluntary organisations, and various other enterprises detailed in later chapters.

For those seeking longer-term employment, or else opting for permanent relocation to Canada, their chances of entry are determined by several varied factors, the most important factor being that of determining whether the individual intends entry on a dependent basis (that is with relatives willing to sponsor his or her entry), or whether that entry is one of independent status, namely the individual seeks approval on the strength of whatever skills, academic and professional qualifications Canada might currently be in need of. Those seeking admission as independents might instead opt for entry on grounds of intending to set up in, or develop already existing businesses, or else to invest in commercial and industrial sectors.

Canada as a highly advanced country, offers job and employment opportunities much on a par with those available in Britain, and consequently those who score highly on the register of skills currently in short supply from amongst Canada's indigenous population, might well find the transferral of skills and qualifications almost hassle free. At other times that transfer from a British to a similar job in Canada might involve specific registration with professional and trade bodies, and might also involve the newcomer serving a probationary period before being admitted as a 'full' member of the profession or trade to which he or she might have belonged for many years.

What is Canada Like to Live In?

Canada's fragmented but doubtless solid nation, is perhaps best described in terms of the varying life styles, laws and conditions that exist in the country's ten provinces and two territories.

One might for instance find jobs aplenty in one region, yet nothing at all by which to earn one's keep in the next. In one province that person whose car features as an easily dispensable luxury might find it proves one of life's more essential possessions in the next province visited.

Population density in Canada is extremely low. Not surprisingly really, for much of this massive continent lies in the frozen wastes, scrub forests and swamplands of the Arctic circle, hardly making for living conditions for which many people would willingly settle. In fact the vast majority of the population (around 80%) lives in a narrow band of towns and cities within 200 kilometres of the shared border with the United States.

For many, the real beauty and magnetism of Canada is those vast open stretches of wasteland – would 'wilderness' be a better and more accurate description – areas in which one can experience life in the raw, and temperatures so low that 'raw' might prove something of an understatement.

In many parts, life resembles almost exactly that of Britain; in such as Quebec one might instead find oneself living in a totally alien environment, other than for those used to living or holidaying in France.

But wherever one's travels lead, a high standard of living awaits the newcomer to this country, which though ranking amongst the top industrialised nations of the world has retained much of its outstanding natural beauty. In Canada there are more waterways and lakes than in any other part of the world.

Surveys carried out over many years, show that very few expatriates regret their decision to live and work in Canada. Those regrets that do surface normally reveal themselves amongst newcomers to the province of Quebec, the overwhelming majority of problems emanating from the divisions between English and French-speaking factions of the community. So strongly do many hold their belief that theirs is a French society, that even where signs are displayed in many foreign languages alongside their French equivalent, it is not unknown for the signpost's erector to be ordered to remove the English translation – only the English translation! A recent article in 'Canada News', relays the story of a store trader who displayed a 'welcome' sign outside his store in 35 different languages. The Quebec 'language police' ordered removal of the English version!

And yet we must not forget that even those without a single word of any other than English at their disposal will face language problems of some description in making the move to Canada. 'Biscuits' are after all 'cookies', and 'lorries' more frequently referred to as 'trucks'.

Canada is in general a 'user friendly' country, where cities and amenities are designed entirely with residents and primarily the weather conditions facing them in mind. One might therefore find the vast majority of shopping expeditions taking place in temperature-controlled shopping malls, and even where one might venture from the upper storeys of one high-rise block to the next, this passage usually takes place via raised enclosed walkways joining buildings, shopping malls, office blocks and so on.

Planners are careful not to compromise the outstanding natural beauty of Canada in the shoppers' quest for bigger and better shopping malls, and hence one discovers wide open spaces, parks, play areas, sports centres and outside sporting facilities dotted liberally around even the busiest of cities. Those keen on keeping their purses intact and their bodies in shape, might instead consider jogging, walking or cycling along the hundreds of miles of specially designated paths networking city centres and suburbs.

Some Pros and Cons

A recent survey undertaken by 'Canada News' shows that the overwhelming majority (approximately 90%) of British expatriates are far more than happy with their decision to opt for life in Canada. The survey revealed that those things Britons most missed about their former homeland were pubs, British history and traditions, country gardens, Sunday newspapers and the BBC.

Of course as for any of life's more important decisions, that choice as to whether or not to move to Canada for whatever period of time, is one the intending tourist, working visitor or potential expatriate should not make without full and careful consideration of all information at his or her disposal about the country itself, its people, life styles, and so on.

Any good book on Canada, alongside information available from Canadian immigration and tourist officials and from ongoing studies such as provided in 'National Geographic', the latter of which is available in bound copies in most main reference libraries, will greatly assist the individual and family in coming to that all important conclusion, 'Should we, or shouldn't we?'

Though we can provide information regarding many of the most commonly expressed advantages and disadvantages of living and working in Canada, the author and publisher of 'Live and Work in Canada' can not help you with your decision. All advantages and disadvantages must be weighed against individual and family preferences.

Consequently in aiding the reader towards making that decision, the following factors are offered:

Arguments for

- Higher standard of living
- Less class consciousness than in Britain
- Lower crime rate and greater sense of personal security
- Cleaner air
- Magnificent scenery and spectacular wide open spaces
- Greater opportunities
- Especially good welfare and social system for retired citizens
- Excellent shopping facilities
- Excellent sports facilities
- The Canadians are an extremely friendly, considerate and hospitable race

Arguments against

- Long, harsh winters
- Language difficulties in some provinces
- Uncertainty in the province of Quebec. French and English factions maintain an ongoing battle for sovereignty. In some instances there can be open hostility toward all things English.

Planning Your Move

That person intending to work in Canada for all but a short period of time, must of course take great pains to determine at the outset whether this is in fact the course best suited to the future well-being of him or herself and family. And by 'family' we mean of course not only those who make that exciting move to life in another land; we must think also of those we leave behind. Those Britons opting for life in nearby France for instance, will find their homesickness cured by the injection of a little cash and a couple of hours to spare for the journey back to Britain; in Canada homesickness and desperation for the well-being of one's relatives back 'home' is a far more costly and time-consuming malady to cure.

Once that decision to go has actually been made, then comes the need to consider options of employment and accommodation. Both decisions will of course be determined by a great many other factors, including adequate and convenient educational facilities, living costs and standards, employment opportunities for other family members, health care standards and costs, recreational facilities, retirement options, unemployment benefits, and so on.

CHAPTER ONE

About Canada – Essential Background Information

What is Canada?

Is it primarily wilderness, or does it instead lend itself more easily to consideration of that broad band of mainly city regions close to the United States, where the majority of Canadians live? Is it very much like England? Does it lend itself better to a way of life more realistically described as 'French'? Do nationals live urbanised life styles? If so, what of those vast open areas of wilderness and spectacular outdoor locations: prairies, mountains, beaches, lakes and forests?

What is Canada then? Any of these things? A few of these things? All of these things, and more? Yes, that latter option best describes this huge and fascinating land.

Canada is divided into two territories: the Yukon and Northwest Territories and ten provinces: Newfoundland, Nova Scotia, Prince Edward Island, New Brunswick, Quebec, Ontario, Manitoba, Alberta, Saskatchewan and British Columbia.

No particular area typifies life in Canada; life and living conditions can vary greatly from one province to the next. One Canadian city might offer life very much on a par with that enjoyed by citizens in any of the major cities of neighbouring United States. Isolation and solitude, busy bustling cities, bitter cold frozen land-masses, warm and sunny endless beaches, a land much like England, a mini version of France – this is Canada!

Quick Geography

This is the world's largest nation, covering an area of 3,849,674 square miles/9,970,6100 square kilometres.

Canada divides into ten provinces and two territories, and covers 40% of the continent of North America.

Seven main geographical regions exist: The **Appalachian** region is an extension of the USA's region of the same name; the **St Lawrence and Lower Great Lakes** region is the country's most densely populated area; the **Canadian (Laurentian) Shield** forms a huge mosaic of ancient rocks, mineral deposits, lakes and rivers. The **Hudson Bay Lowland** forms a plain between the Canadian Shield and Hudson Bay. **Western Interior Plains** lie between the Shield and the **Western Mountains**, the latter of which contain the Rockies and the Coast Range. To the extreme north are the **Arctic** regions, a mass of bleak desolate islands.

Stretching downwards from the Arctic ocean, and across from Pacific to Atlantic, Canada covers as widely diversified a topography as one is ever likely to encounter: prairies, mountains, lakes, rocky regions and forest, the latter of which cover approximately 35% of the country's entire land surface. Almost 40% of Canada falls within the Arctic region.

Interior lowlands occupy approximately 80% of land surface. Here is located the extensive Canadian Shield, the St. Lawrence-Great Lakes lowlands and the interior plains.

Weather and Climate

As is the case for all large countries, Canada's climate differs widely from one region to the next. Long severe winters characterise the Arctic regions, whilst primarily cool temperate, near continental conditions prevail in southern parts.

In the north, Arctic winters are harsh not only for reasons of latitude, but because much of the area exists at heights of up to 20,000 feet above sea level. Ocean influences contribute further to a climate that renders many areas totally devoid of inhabitants – of the human variety that is! And to make matters worse, there are periods of 24 hours darkness to contribute to already appalling weather conditions. A great deal of the time, inhabitants must hack away at icebergs and frozen lakes before they can acquire sufficient material to melt in readiness for domestic consumption.

Generally however, Canada experiences long winters which though often bitterly cold are usually dry; spring is usually short but mild; summers though quite warm last for only two or three months, and autumn usually proves refreshingly clear and crisp.

But it is the sheer depth to which Canada's winter temperatures can sink that lies at the very root of many British expatriates' decisions to return home to Britain. Winter though cold and windy in Quebec and the Rocky mountains, has little on those temperatures for which the Yukon and Northwest territories are renowned, and which can find temperatures dropping to – 16°F. The Yukon actually boasts an all-time low temperature of – 81°F.

In the prairies spring comes late, usually after a long period in which the crisp snows of winter have given way to a dirty slushy aftermath. Summer though can brighten those grey days quite significantly, with temperatures often reaching 30 degrees centigrade and over.

In central Canada, seasonal variations closely resemble those of the prairie regions, but with a more humid atmosphere very much in evidence. Autumn in this part of the world is perhaps more spectacular than anywhere else on earth, as maple trees create a colourful thick blanket to walk over, drive over, or simply just marvel over.

Along the Pacific coast, rainfall is at its highest, decreasing the further inland one travels. The opposite is true of summer temperatures, which though often fairly high in inland areas, decrease rapidly en route to coastal regions.

Rainfall in British Columbia on the south-west coast is amongst the world's highest, where several locations register annual falls of over 100 inches. Vancouver experiences an annual rainfall averaging close to 41 inches. In Montreal rainfall averages 41 inches; in Toronto one encounters a far lower 30 inches.

In the north and prairie regions, rainfall drops to an almost insignificant 15 inches, mainly because of coastal mountains providing shelter from sea breezes.

Canada has come to terms with its often harsh climate, developing a user-friendly society that provides citizens with underpasses and overpasses between buildings and thoroughfares; even underground shopping malls, some complete with hotels, cinemas, bowling parks, restaurants, and an extensive range of leisure facilities.

The Canadian Outlook

Canadians are fiercely proud of their country and take great exception to being considered, albeit innocently, as part and parcel of the American populace, even though around 80% of them live within 200 kilometres of their Country's border with the United States. Even so, Canadians tend on the whole to be less rowdy than their southern neighbours, opting instead for a slower pace to life, and presenting an image of courtesy and quiet respect to nationals and expatriates alike.

One of Canada's main problems stems from her multi-cultural origins which culminates in ongoing disputes and hassles between descendants of English and French speaking nationals, each claiming their own is the 'natural' language of their 'new' country. To ease the tension a little, law demands that all packaging, government documents, street signs and such be printed in both languages. A little superfluous a measure perhaps, and one more likely designed to gloss over the issue, since most Canadians are in fact bilingual.

There is perhaps for obvious reasons, no truly stereotyped image of the 'average' Canadian; such a person does not exist. Canadians have roots stemming from a wide range of ethnic origins; their culture and traditions are as varied and constantly mutating as one is ever likely to come by, considering the warm welcome Canada has given, and continues to give, to nationals from foreign lands. And given the wide geographical distances between many populated regions, one can find great differences in life styles and attitudes from one city to the next; more markedly so between individual provinces.

What can be said of Canadians however, is that in general they are a gregarious and happy-go-lucky group, reserved and respectful of authority, fond of city life but ever-mindful of the fantastic opportunities awaiting them out of doors whether as spectators of magnificent scenery, or participants in the many sporting and leisure facilities available to them.

Religion

Overwhelmingly Christian in denomination, almost half of the population belongs to the Roman Catholic faith (47%). Large groups are represented by the Protestant Church and the United Church of Canada; small minority religious groups include Muslim, Jewish, Sikh and Hindu.

Language

Canada's official languages: English (63%) and French (25%) testify to the origins of the vast majority of inhabitants. In Quebec, French is the official language. Although in certain parts of the country one finds pockets where one or other of these official languages is spoken exclusively, a great many Canadians have taken the obvious advantages of bilingual speech.

All governmental, legal and main business decisions and communications are published in both languages; radio, television and newspaper industries follow suit. In addition, law demands that all government documentation, product packaging and information of general interest be printed in both official languages.

In reality English tends to predominate in most parts of Canada, and though to the untrained ear the Canadian accent might seem to have a great deal in common with that of the United States, in written form Canadian English is very much closer to the original; 'labour' and 'centre' for instance stand out as very much alien to their American counterparts' 'labor' and 'center'.

To confuse matters just a little further, in Newfoundland one discovers a dialect bearing uncanny resemblance to the Irish.

And given provincials' ardent claims for separatism and allegiance to all things French, in Quebec the traveller finds his or her chances of acceptance all that much enhanced with just a token attempt to converse or otherwise communicate with the locals in French. French as the primary language becomes somewhat watered down the further one travels from Quebec and a few other pockets of dominant French-speaking communities dotted throughout Canada. 'Francophone' is the term given to French-speaking regions and peoples, 'Anglophone' that label accorded to advocates of English.

And perhaps surprisingly, even those arriving in Quebec with fluency in French to back them up, might find themselves more than a little troubled in understanding and interpreting 'Quebecois', which with time has altered significantly from that language as originally imported into Canada. Many English words have mixed with the French to form a unique combination of 'false friends' whose definition is almost certainly known only to long standing inhabitants of the province.

Native Amerindian languages survive amongst almost 100,000 of the population, the majority of whom speak Cree, Ojibway and Inuktitut (Eskimo).

Brief History

Canada's first inhabitants were Asian Indians whose transition between continents over 40,000 years ago, was facilitated by ice and land bridge over what subsequently became the Bering Straits. The descendants of these ancient explorers live on in Canada's Eskimo and Inuit populations.

The earliest of Canada's now overwhelmingly 'European' population were Vikings who arrived in Newfoundland during the 11th century. It was to be several hundred years before further European settlements would be founded in Canada, when in 1497 the Italian sailor John Cabot, acting on behalf of the British, landed in Newfoundland.

Over three decades later it was the turn of the French to discover and claim part of this massive land for their own King, to whom was accorded sovereignty over the St Lawrence River basin region. Jacques Cartier, leader of the expedition, believing he had discovered a passage to the Orient, continued his travels down the St. Lawrence river until he ventured upon ancient Iroquois villages which would eventually become Montreal and Quebec City.

Quebec itself was founded by Samuel de Champlain in 1604, followed soon by intense rivalry between the French and British. Between 1689 and 1763 Britain conquered the French settlements, and in 1867 (The Year of Confederation), the Dominion of Canada, comprising Quebec, Ontario, Nova Scotia and New Brunswick was established. Amalgamation with other provinces continued from 1870 to as late as 1949 when Newfoundland also sought inclusion.

Clashes between French and British factions began as early as 1686, the dispute then centring on the overlapping of their respective fur-trading operations. Squabbles continued on an almost relentless basis, until peace of albeit minor proportions, was reached with the signing of the Treaty of Utrecht in 1713, with certain rights and restrictions applied to both parties. Clashes between those of French and British origins today (approximately 27% and 40% of citizens respectively) focus largely on the subject of language, and centre primarily in and around Quebec.

War declared between France and England in the mid-17th century did nothing to preserve what relative peace the Treaty of Utrecht had afforded, when both nations sent their troops to preserve and protect their respective rights in Canada. Following defeat of the French on the Plains of Abraham, under the Treaty of Paris (1763), France surrendered all of her lands in Canada to the British.

The American civil war and threats to invade Canada, led to steps being taken to increase the British population in Canada; free land was therefore offered to new immigrants. Throughout the 19th century immigrants arrived in their millions. Despite such incentives, early 20th century Canada remained a sparsely populated continent, something which prompted the government to venture further afield in its quest for immigrants to this new and prosperous land.

In return for a guarantee to remain in Canada for a minimum six months, immigrants received large spreads of prairie grassland entirely free of charge, other that is than for a ten dollars registration fee required of them. So high was the level of 'takers' that two new provinces – Alberta and Saskatchewan – were created to cater for them.

Canada's independence was finally recognized in the Statute of Westminster, 1931, when the former British colony became a fully independent sovereign state within the British Commonwealth. Depression in the 1930s all but disabled many parts of Canada; Newfoundland fell into bankruptcy.

A major force in World War II and the Korean War, Canada was a founder member of NATO.

The ferocity with which many Canadians remain loyal to their French roots, has been the cause of great tension and disharmony. In the 1970s and 80s, so strong did the argument for sovereignty of the French language become, that in such as Quebec separatism became a very real issue, although in a referendum in 1980 only 40% voted for separatism. The argument with Quebec continues to this day, although now exponents of Canada's official languages tend to opt for a far more conciliatory attitude towards their differences.

On April 17th, 1982, an Act of Parliament proclaimed by Queen Elizabeth II, formally ceded all British control over Canada, thereby finally accepting the latter's responsibility for its own constitution.

Government

Canada is a federal state whose capital is Ottawa, Ontario.

There are three levels of government in existence: federal, provincial and municipal, each financed through different taxation systems paid by residents. Such taxes include federal income tax, a Goods and Services tax, municipal property tax, and in the majority of provinces a retail sales tax system is in force. Each level of government is elected by popular democratic vote.

National (federal) government is the responsibility of the Canadian Parliament, consisting of two houses: a Senate of 104 members appointed by the Governor General to represent the various provinces, and a House of Commons consisting of 295 members elected democratically for a five-year period. Senate, very much in common with Britain's House of Lords, has very little real power and serves similarly to ratify and to some extent qualify decisions of the 'lower' house.

The Prime Minister, whose appointment is ratified by the Governor General representing the British Queen as titular head of state, leads a majority party in the House of Commons. The Queen and Governor General exist purely as figure-heads, with actual power resting entirely in a Prime Minister whose main function it is to appoint and head a Cabinet of Ministers responsible to the House of Commons.

Provinces additionally have their own locally-administered government and legislatures, responsible for property and civil codes, education systems, marriage licences, working conditions, health care and social services, civil law and some criminal law, local government and direct taxation within their own boundaries.

In each province there is a lieutenant-governor who acts as representative of the governor general. An elected legislature and executive council headed by a premier, exercises considerable control by virtue of decentralization of federal authority.

Complete power is shared between national and provincial governments, the former of which is based in Ottawa. Federal government is solely responsible for matters of national concern, including defence, trade and foreign affairs, banking and commerce, the postal services, navigation and shipping, the criminal legal system and fisheries.

Local (Municipal) Government

Individual communities are governed by municipal authorities, responsible for such as police and fire protection, local courts and jails, sanitation and hygiene, snow removal, road maintenance and local public health services.

Politics

Canada's main political parties are the Liberal Party, The Progressive Conservative Party and the New Democratic (Socialist) Party.

The present conservative government came to power in February 1990, headed by prime minister Brian Mulroney.

Voting is by universal suffrage.

Politically, Canada is a well balanced and stable country. Parties favour a system of free market economy, although many service industries remain under government control or supervision.

The Economy

Canada boasts one of the world's highest standards of living, a fact due primarily to her vast mineral reserves. Zinc, nickel, gold, silver, iron ore, uranium, copper, cobalt and lead reserves are plentiful, as are those of petroleum and natural gas.

Principal mining regions are in the provinces of Alberta, British Columbia, Saskatchewan and Quebec.

A census carried out in 1986 revealed that agricultural land takes up 168 million acres. Over 75% of cultivable land is located in the Western Canadian prairies, where grain, dairying, fruit, fur farming and ranching are flourishing industries. Forestry accounts for approximately 10% of Canada's employment, mainly occupied in producing lumber and newsprint.

Major industries growing up around Canada's huge reserves of forested and agricultural land, include: lumber, pulp, paper, plywood, farming, along with numerous other sectors including fishing, petroleum refining, mining and motor vehicle production.

Canada is amongst the world's major exporters of cereals, primarily wheat from the country's vast prairie regions. Amongst other cereals grown in great abundance in this country's wide open regions are: barley, oats and rye. Abundant land surface yields plentiful supplies of fruits, beef and potatoes.

And from her long Pacific and Atlantic shores Canada boasts proud claim as the world's leading exporter of fish and seafood. Main sea products are salmon, cod, lobster and herring.

Minerals and energy are vital components of the export trade, this being a major producer of uranium, potash, asbestos, oil, gas and hydroelectricity. In the eastern prairies, farming predominates. Throughout the country, manufacturing assumes vital importance to the economy, included amongst the major industrial sectors are such as: petroleum refining, vehicle manufacture, and machine and equipment manufacturing. Electronic and computer companies have emerged rapidly in recent years.

Business centres primarily on banking, insurance and real estate, and of course in so unspoilt a country, tourism features highly on the agenda; the latter makes up over 5% of GNP and employs around 10% of the workforce.

Canada's impressive industrial growth rate (5.7% in 1988), is almost entirely due to the continued success of its mineral industry and ongoing efforts to expand the manufacturing sector.

Traditionally a trading nation, the majority of transactions take place with the United States, followed by the British Commonwealth, Japan, and Russia.

Canada exports in excess of $120 billion of products annually, and imports goods to the value of approximately $110 billion. The United States and Canada, so alike in many other ways, also compliment one another as principal trading partners. Growing export links between Canada and the United States have lessened trading links with other parts of the world, a fact that can perhaps best be explained in terms of geographical proximity than any other factor.

Amongst her main contributions to the requirements of the British are: cork and wood; metal ores and scrap; transport equipment; paper and paperboard; power generating machinery; non-ferrous metals; pulp and waste paper.

Major imports include processed foods, beverages, crude petroleum, chemicals, industrial machinery, motor vehicles and electronic computers.

The 1988 budget was for expenditure of US$89,500 million and revenue of US$75,200 million. Main items of expenditure are housing and welfare (36%); health (6.3%); defence (8.1%).

The Future

The future for Canada looks set to continue on the same upwards trend to which nationals have become accustomed.

Recently accorded the title of 'World's best place in which to live' by a survey carried out by the UN, living standards look set if not to rise, then at least to continue at that high standard currently envied the world over.

Canada's aging population might however have some influence upon the size and suitability of tomorrow's labourforce, perhaps also reflecting itself in immigration levels, qualifications, and professions designated suitable for entry.

Problems do however, look set to continue between French and English factions, each dedicated – not unnaturally – to the language, traditions, views and customs of their ancestors. But despite occasional flare-ups that characterise life in such as Quebec, it must be said that what problems and disagreements exist, rarely give way to extreme acts of violence or insurmountable problems for those caught up in the dispute.

Economically, Canada's vast reserve of natural resources are as yet largely untapped, surely making for a stability the remainder of the world will remain continuously and deeply envious of.

Cities, Towns and Population

Official figures place the population at almost 27 million, of which over three-quarters live in urban areas.

Of those 27 million inhabitants, the largest ethnic group is of British extraction (around 40%), followed closely by those of French origins. The remainder are largely of Italian, Ukranian, Chinese, German, Dutch and Polish extraction. Native races – Eskimo and Indian tribes – form a very tiny, almost insignificant proportion of the population. Of less than 2% of inhabitants, Dene (Indians) number around 300,000 people; Inuits (Eskimos) approximately 23,000. The majority of native people live on reservations in Ontario and in the four western provinces, notably Saskatchewan.

Poverty, unemployment and deprivation are the most common features of life confronting these indigenous races, for whom solace seems to come more commonly in the shape of the alcohol bottle than in any hard-fought and universal campaign for reform. Very few natives have made their way into everyday society, although one frequently finds a lawyer or accountant of Indian or Eskimo extraction. Sadly, the majority of their fellows who have attempted the transition from reservation to city life are usually to be found on street corners, shabbily dressed, and with bottle in hand. Few of their native traditions are in evidence; very few dress in their traditional costume; some have little recognisable knowledge of their native tongue.

Canada's population is very unevenly distributed, and in many parts there exist vast areas totally devoid of habitation.

Some 80% or so of Canada's population is to be found in the provinces of Quebec, Ontario, Alberta and British Columbia. Conversely, though covering one third of the country's entire land surface, the Yukon and Northwest Territories are home to only a tiny 0.3% of the population. Approximately 80% of the population is concentrated into a thin ribbon of land skirting the border with the United States.

Major Towns and Cities, and respective population figures (1989) are as follows:

Ottawa (Capital)	819,300
Toronto	3,427,200
Montreal	2,921,400
Vancouver	1,380,700
Edmonton	785,500
Calgary	671,300
Winnipeg	625,300
Quebec	603,300
Hamilton	557,000

Official records of 1989 featured the following population statistics:

Birth Rate 1.52%
Death Rate 0.71%
Rate of Population Increase (1980 – 87) 0.81%
Life expectancy – Female = 80; Male = 73: Average = 77

Where to Live in Canada

Canada, given its sheer size, presents a great many factors that must be taken into account in deciding where to make one's home. The fact that habitation ranges from nil to but a few thousand individuals in some parts of the frozen north, whilst 80% of the population inhabits that narrow band where Canada shares borders with the United States, must surely speak volumes for those places known to produce the most promising, comfortable and enjoyable of life styles.

But it isn't of course purely to the likes of temperature, scenery, leisure activities, and such that one must make that vitally important decision as to exactly where to live. Jobs opportunities; specific labour shortages in particular provinces; proximity or otherwise to major cities; a preference for a predominantly 'French' or alternatively 'English' way of life; these and a great many other factors also come into play when deciding that part of Canada in which to settle.

In fact, as an intending migrant, certain provinces might not enter into the deliberations when considering whether you and your family will be allowed entry into Canada. Many provinces are adequately staffed with employees of a job or profession for which a neighbouring province might be experiencing a great shortage of suitable staff. Consequently it might be primarily the labour market upon which your entry or refusal for entry will be determined.

A Brief Overview of Priority Factors

For most job opportunities: Manitoba, British Columbia, Quebec, Ontario, Saskatchewan

For most industrial job opportunities: Manitoba, British Columbia

For best foreign investment opportunities: British Columbia, Manitoba, Toronto

For most commercial job opportunities: Ottawa, Toronto, Montreal, Vancouver

For most high-tech job opportunities: Ontario, British Columbia, Toronto, Ottawa

For attractive scenery: Virtually everywhere. British Columbia is particularly rich in national and provincial parks (approximately 400), icefields, lakes, snow-capped mountains

For cosmopolitan, 'big city' atmosphere: Vancouver, Toronto

'English' locations: Victoria, Nova Scotia, parts of Toronto

'French' locations: Quebec, Montreal

Busiest and best social life: Toronto, Vancouver, Montreal, Ottawa

To experience various cultures: Toronto, Quebec, Montreal, Nova Scotia, Northwest Territories

Busy city life: Vancouver, Toronto, Ottawa

Busy city life but with slow pace of life nearby (for those who want it)**:** Vancouver, Victoria, Toronto, Winnipeg, Ottawa

Special Note:

Recent surveys have placed Montreal and Toronto as the most expensive parts of Canada in which to live; both cities also feature near the top of the list of the world's most expensive cities.

City by City and Region by Region

How to Use This Section

Those set on enjoying their lives in Canada, whether that visit in intended as one of but a few weeks, months or lifelong duration, owe it to themselves to learn as much about this fascinating and spectacularly beautiful country as they are able in advance of venturing from their present homeland.

A wealth of information is available to guide the tourist or intending migrant through the maze of opportunities, places to visit, varying life styles and whatever else he or she might need or want to know about visiting, living and possibly working in Canada. Most such information is available from Canadian tourist offices in Britain and Canada, along with many other publications available in book stores and by mail from appropriate publishers.

Canada comprises two territories: the Northwest Territories and Yukon, and ten provinces: Newfoundland, Nova Scotia, Prince Edward Island, New Brunswick, Quebec, Ontario, Manitoba, Alberta, Saskatchewan and British Columbia.

Territories

THE NORTHWEST TERRITORIES

These comprise all the land north of the 60th parallel between Hudson Bay and the Yukon, including the islands of Hudson Bay and James Bay, along with all Arctic islands. Given the long, hard and intensely cold conditions prevailing in this region, not surprisingly only one per cent of Canada's entire population is located in an area which covers over one-third of land surface. This tiny population is overwhelmingly Eskimo.

Despite the problems one will encounter in terms of isolation and harsh weather conditions, here the visitor is likely to encounter some of the most spectacular of Canadian scenery, ranging from extensive ocean coastlines, tundra and polar desert regions; to the untamed beauty of two of the world's largest lakes, Great Bear and Great Slave, and on to Virginia Falls, twice the height of Niagara.

Key Facts

Area: 1,304,903 square miles/3,379,285 square kilometres
Population: 55,000
Capital: Yellowknife

Note: In 1990 an agreement was reached for the division of the Northwest Territories into two separate territories: Nunavut in the east where an Eskimo (Inuit) majority exists, and Nenedeh Territory in the west, home to a primarily indigenous Indian community.

Points of Interest

Information Services

The Government of the Northwest Territories issues an annual 'Explorers' Guide', in which are listed hotels, lodges, restaurants, and all essential information for tourists and residents. Copies can be obtained from:

TravelArctic,
Yellowknife, North West Territories, XOE 1HO.

Accommodation

Almost all communities have one hotel or Inuit co-operative. Full details on 'Explorers' Guide' – see above.

Getting There/Getting Around

By Air – Canadian Airlines International fly regularly between Edmonton/Winnipeg to Yellowknife. Domestic services operate via Northwest Territorial Airways, based in Yellowknife.

By Rail – no passenger rail service to Northwest Territories.

By Bus – Canadian Coachways and NWT Coachlines Ltd., operate various services between Edmonton and Yellowknife.

By Car – Two main highways. One of them, the Mackenzie Highway runs between Edmonton, Alberta and Yellowknife. For driving conditions see 'By Car' in the following section – The Yukon.

Main Newspaper

News North

Miscellaneous

Legal drinking age is 19 years. Bars close at 1 am. Many parts are completely dry by law.

Useful Addresses

Tourist Office

Department of Economic Development and Tourism,
Yellowknife, Canada, X1A 2L9.

THE YUKON TERRITORY

The Yukon is that heavily forested area to which much of Canada's flourishing logging industry owes its existence.

One of the saddest facts is that in this vast and sparsely populated area to which very few tourists venture, perhaps the most magnificent scenery Canada has to offer remains virtually unknown to the outside world. Mountains, valleys, plateaus and rivers, and the Kluane National Park are but a few of the 'once seen, never forgotten' sights of the Yukon.

And in Dawson, the centre of that infamous gold rush in which millionaires were almost overnight relieved of their pauper's rags, legalised gambling still exists, alongside a live vaudeville theatre, and the raucous 'Gertie's' floor show, complete with entertainment provided by can-can girls and honky-tonk piano players. History might truly be said to live on in Dawson.

Key Facts

Area: 186,299 square miles/482,515 square kilometres
Population: 30,000
Capital: Whitehorse

Points of Interest

Information Services

Tourism Yukon publishes a booklet 'Come on in to Canada's Yukon', in which are detailed lodgings and restaurants, road maps, and other essential travel information. Copies can be obtained from:

Tourism Yukon,
Box 2703, Whitehorse, Yukon, Y1A 2C6.

Accommodation

A good range of facilities are available at most price levels. See booklet available from 'Tourism Yukon', mentioned earlier.

Getting There/Getting Around

By Air – CP Air flies from Edmonton and Vancouver to Whitehorse. Domestic services are provided by range of small carriers and charter operators.

By Rail – A railway line links Whitehorse and Skagway, Alaska.

By Bus – Greyhound Buses and Coachways operate services between Edmonton and Whitehorse, as well as providing a limited domestic service.

By Car – Several major highways exist. The speed limit is 80 kph (50 mph). Main roads are gravelled, and though officially open all year round, are usually impassible between November and May/ June. Specific rules and legal regulations apply to travel in the North West Territories and the Yukon, including the requirement that headlights must remain on at all times, headlights should be protected by plastic covers from gravel chips thrown up from roads, motorists should refill petrol tanks regularly, and no long journeys should be undertaken without careful and early planning.

Main Newspaper
Whitehorse Star

Miscellaneous
Minimum drinking age is 19 years; closing time is 2 am.

Useful Addresses

Tourist Office

Tourism Yukon,
PO Box 2703, Whitehorse, Canada, Y1A 2C6.

The Provinces

The **Western** provinces include the prairie regions of British Columbia, Saskatchewan, Alberta and Manitoba.

BRITISH COLUMBIA
Area: 366,255 square miles/948,596 square kilometres
Capital: Victoria
Largest City: Vancouver

Rich in snow-capped mountains (including the Rockies), national and provincial parks (around 400 of them), icefields, crystal lakes and river valleys, it is to its huge forest regions that British Columbia boasts a truly massive and exceedingly wealthy timber industry. Here is produced around one quarter of all timber sold in North America. Mining features highly mainly in the Cordillero region rich in lead, zinc and silver. Valuable fish reserves are exploited along the province's extensive Pacific shores.

Captain Cook is credited with the discovery of Canada's westernmost province in the late 1700s. British interest in the area quickly became apparent and less than a century later the British crown colony of Vancouver Island came into being.

Colonisation of the province by the British did not take place until almost two decades later, when gold discovered on the Fraser River prompted the move to extend sovereignty over those areas in which treasure trove was most likely to exist.

British Columbia is home to people of many different ethnic origins, ranging from various parts of Europe to Africa, and on to almost all countries of Asia, to say nothing of those from parts of that overall land mass of the 'Americas'.

British Columbia covers a land surface almost four times the size of Britain, and shares borders with the American states of Washington, Idaho and Montana.

This is a province in which industry and business opportunities are in plentiful supply, an area that suffered less than others at the hands of the recession Canada is hopefully now pulling out of. For these reasons, British Columbia is one of the most attractive provinces for foreign investment.

Largest city Vancouver, often mistaken for capital of this province, is not as one might easily suppose, actually located on Vancouver Island, but is to be found instead on the mainland. Much smaller, but nevertheless capital of the province, it is the scenic city of Victoria that boasts status as prime city of Vancouver Island.

Points of Interest

Information Services

Tourism BC, the tourist office address for which is listed under 'Useful Addresses', publishes the 'British Columbia Accommodations Guide', in which are listed all accommodation services available in the province.

Main Newspaper

Vancouver Sun

Useful Addresses

Tourist Office

Tourism British Columbia,
Parliament Buildings, Victoria, V8V 1X4.

UK Tourist Office (British Columbia),
British Columbia House, 1 Regent Street, London, SW1Y 4NS.

Ferry Services are provided by:

British Columbia Ferry Corporation,
Vancouver.

ALBERTA

Area: 255,285 square miles/661,199 square kilometres
Capital: Edmonton

Approximately 50% of people live in Calgary and Edmonton.

A prairie state, much of the country's grain and cereal originates here. Oil, coal and gas industries are the region's major employers. Alberta produces in excess of 10% of the nation's petrochemical products.

But it is to the sheer beauty of the Rockie mountains of her western reaches that most people believe Alberta owes her fame. Here there are four national parks, home to magnificent lakes, chateaux, and huge stretches of land dedicated entirely to outdoor pursuits: picnicking, camping, hiking, are but a few of the opportunities available to the lover of the great outdoors. It is in fact to the excellent skiing facilities Alberta has to offer that this province is renowned amongst outdoor enthusiasts; miles and miles of ski runs, laden in deep dry powder 'masquerading' as snow, along with countless sunny days, all no doubt explain Alberta's other title, namely that of 'skier's paradise'.

Capital city Edmonton, lies in the very heart of the prairies, and has earned the well-deserved title 'festival city', due to a series of summer festivals in which streets and parks fill to over-flowing. Primary amongst these festivals, and certainly those no self-respecting tourist or resident would choose to miss, are the festivals of Jazz City International and Klondike Days.

Also in Edmonton one finds the world famous West Edmonton shopping mall, home to over 800 shops, with respite for weary shoppers offered in a myriad of movie theatres. Also available to those tiring of everyday shopping are a magnificent waterpark, and the world's largest indoor amusement park, all a far cry away from that with which the shopper in Britain is usually familiar.

Calgary, a modern city of around three-quarters of a million residents, basks under the alternative name of 'Oil Capital of the West'. Another beautiful city, which though home to ultra-modern skyscrapers and modern efficient railway systems, boasts a number of desirable residential suburbs which prove a popular destination for the newcomer to Canada.

Points of Interest

Information Services

Alberta Provincial government publishes a regularly updated 'Visitor's Accommodation Guide', in which are listed approved hotels, motels, camp sites, resort areas. Another publication 'Adventure Guide' provides essential information concerning travel and sight-seeing excursions, road maps, etc. Information is available from the Travel Alberta office listed under the following section 'Useful Addresses'.

Main Newspapers

Alberta Journal
Calgary Herald

Useful Addresses

Tourist Offices

Travel Alberta,
10025 Jasper Avenue, 15th Floor, Edmonton, T5J 3Z3.

The Calgary Tourist and Convention Association,
Hospitality Center, 237 8th Avenue, Calgary.

Edmonton Convention and Tourism Authority,
104, 9799 Jasper Avenue, Edmonton, T5J 1N9.

Alberta Tourism (British Office),
Alberta House, 1 Mount Street, London, W1Y 5AA. 071 491 3430

SASKATCHEWAN

Area: 251,700 square miles/651,900 square kilometres
Capital: Regina
Largest City: Saskatoon

This is Canada's primary wheat growing region. Also featuring highly in the economy and employment of inhabitants are rearing of livestock, and mining of gold, silver and cadmium.

Capital city Regina, until chosen late in the nineteenth century as capital of Saskatchewan took the far less regal title, 'Pile o' Bones', something which was hastily rectified by choosing a name more befitting its benefactor Queen Victoria. Regina is the home of the Royal Canadian Mounted Police (RCMP) academy, the Centennial museum and the elaborate architecture of the RCMP chapel, the latter the city's oldest building.

In summer the province is transformed into a tourist's paradise, with over 55 families in the southern part of the province operating vacation farms, where tourists can enjoy living and working alongside the families, or else can turn to the less active spectator sport of rodeo watching. A rodeo circuit covers the province, providing so many events that it is difficult to find a day free of entertainment for visitors and locals.

Main Newspaper

Leader-Post

Useful Addresses

Tourist Office

Tourism Saskatchewan,
1919 Saskatchewan Drive, Regina, Saskatchewan, S4P 3V7.

MANITOBA

Area: 251,000 square miles/650,087 square kilometres
Capital: Winnipeg

Another great prairie state, over half of the province's total one million people is concentrated into capital city Winnipeg.

Winnipeg itself ranks as one of the world's best cities, not only for scenery, architecture, preservation and promotion of the arts, and a wide selection of leisure opportunities available to residents, but also because it functions equally well as a centre of commerce, banking and railroading.

Manitoba is renowned for the warmth and hospitality of its residents, a blend of individuals descended from virtually every country and continent of the world. The province also boasts a workforce amongst the most satisfied of any region in Canada. Manitoba in fact has one of the lowest unemployment rates in the country, a factor perhaps owing much to a stable economy built on a wide diversity of agricultural, industrial, forestry, mining and service industry sectors. Job, business and investment opportunities abound in this province which has lost less time to strikes and labour relations conflicts than has any other province.

Points of Interest

Information Services

'Manitoba Vacation Guide' is the title of a free guide issued by the provincial government, in which are listed accommodation facilities, camp sites, places of interest, tour operators, and so on. This essential guide can be obtained from Travel Manitoba offices, the main one of which is listed in the following section 'Useful Addresses'.

Main Newspaper

Winnipeg Free Press

Useful Addresses

Tourist Office

Travel Manitoba,
7th floor, 155 Carlton Street, Winnipeg MB, Canada, R3C 3H8.

In the **Central** provinces lie Ontario and Quebec.

ONTARIO

Area: 412,582 square miles/1,068,582 square kilometres.
Capital: Toronto

A massive province, around 90% of land surface is dominated by dense green forests. The majority of inhabitants concentrate along the southern border regions. Toronto is located on the shores of Lake Ontario, and is the political, financial and cultural centre of Canada.

Ontario is the most industrialized of all provinces, and here one can be forgiven for assuming this is part of the United States, since the province is buried geographically deep into the northern reaches of its neighbour in the lower section of the Canadian mainland. Certainly its location brings a more 'American' atmosphere to the population and their way of life, lending also a blend of sophistication and power perhaps unknown in any other part of Canada.

Here we find the spectacular Niagara Falls, that majestic point at which Lake Erie overflows into Lake Ontario at the rate of 35,000 cubic litres a second, or as Canadian tourist information puts it 'one million bathtubs of water every second'. 'Second' wonder of the Ontarian world is the CN Tower in Toronto, which at 1,815 feet (457m) is the world's tallest free standing structure.

The waters of the Falls though, are not the only ones for which the province is renowned, for here there are over 400,000 lakes, bounded by spectacular scenery, rolling hills and forests, almost all within easy reach of major cities.

Bustling city centres belie the fact that close by life takes on a far slower pace; not far from the crowds one finds some of the world's most spectacular lakes, forests and wildlife parks.

Points of Interest

Information Services

Travel and tourism offices issue an excellent range of booklets for all visitors to Ontario.

Main Newspapers

Toronto Globe and MailThe Toronto Star

Useful Addresses

Tourist Offices

Ontario Ministry of Tourism,
77 Bloor St. W, 9th Floor, Toronto, M7A 2K9.

National Arts Center,
18 Byward Market Street, Ottawa.

Ontario Tourism (British Office),
21 Knightsbridge, London, SW1X 7LY.

QUEBEC

Area: 594,860 square miles/1,540,680 square kilometres
Capital: Quebec
Largest City: Montreal

This is Canada's largest province and focus of its French population. Over half of Quebec is covered in lakes, rivers and dense green forest regions, the latter wherein paper and paper-processing industries thrive. Mining of gold and asbestos industries are located throughout the province. Fishing, cereal and dairy products are also of great importance to the province.

Montreal, situated on the St. Lawrence river, is Quebec's largest city, and home to the country's oldest European population, overwhelmingly French in character.

Separatism between French and English is a very real issue in Quebec, and something though long held at bay by the authorities, has found the United Church of Canada recently lending its might in favour of a split. What will come of its support is anyone's guess; until now the issue though failing only marginally to win the vote of the electorate, has proved amenable to government placation – perhaps some would more appropriately suggest a glossing over of the issue – by means of laws and regulations passed to protect and promote the French language and culture.

Points of Interest

Information Services

The province is divided into 18 Touristic Associations, each of which can offer a wide range of information regarding accommodation, eating and leisure facilities, places of interest, and so on. See the following section 'Useful Addresses' for details.

Main Newspapers

Le Journal de Montreal
The Quebec Chronicle Telegraph

Useful Addresses

Tourist Office

Tourisme Quebec,
Case Postale 20000, Quebec, PQ Canada, GIK 7X2.

Tourisme Quebec,
2 Place Ville Marie, Montreal.

Tourisme Quebec,
12 rue St Anne, Quebec City.

Convention and Tourist Bureau of Greater Montreal,
Place Bonaventure, Montreal.

Tourism Quebec (British Office),
59 Pall Mall, London, SW1Y 5JH.

The Eastern (Atlantic) provinces comprise several provinces, in which, given the huge coastal regions surrounding the mainland and archipelago regions, the major industry is fishing. This is perhaps the least prosperous part of Canada, not a situation that is likely to be rectified by the outdated fishing and farming techniques one encounters in the region.

Life takes on a slow pace in the Atlantic provinces, almost as though time has stood still for a century or more. But though one finds the locals not averse to complaining that their problems owe much to what they see as federal government turning a blind eye to their plight, it is also true to say that inhabitants are in the main a peace-loving people who would even, given opportunities for change, no doubt continue with their time-honoured old-fashioned ways.

NEW BRUNSWICK

Area: 28,354 square miles/73,437 square kilometres
Capital: Fredericton
Largest City: St. John

In New Brunswick 85% of land surface is forested, again supporting a thriving paper and paper-processing industry. The forests camouflage and often impede access to a region rich in lead, copper and zinc.

Fishing assumes paramount importance in New Brunswick.

Fredericton, the 'City of Stately Elms', is home to a large French population; French is the 'native' tongue of around one third of New Brunswick's inhabitants.

Life in New Brunswick is not completely behind the times, for largest city St. John, Canada's oldest city, located on the banks of the Bay of Fundy lays claim to the first police force in North America, as well as first newspaper and first bank in Canada.

Life though is not steeped entirely in history; there is much for today's high fliers to enjoy, almost all of it out of doors. The province is bordered on three sides by the ocean, providing a unique opportunity to participate in whale-watching and also the activities of seals, dolphins and other, sometimes rarer specimens of wildlife.

New Brunswick in fact offers as widely diversified a range of geographical regions as one might find in any other part of Canada, ranging from long scenic rivers, to rugged cliffs, rolling countryside and breath-taking woodland regions, sandy beaches and coastal regions, to small quiet towns and villages so appealing to photographers, tourists and nationals alike.

Not all in New Brunswick is as quiet as those backwater towns and villages might suggest, for here one might enjoy the magic of year-long fairs, festivals and whatever other overcrowded celebratory gatherings one can imagine.

Points of Interest

Information Services

Tourist offices issue a wide range of information relating to accommodation, travel facilities, places of interest, road maps, and much more essential information for tourists and residents alike. See 'Useful Addresses'.

Tourism New Brunswick operates a 'Dial-a-Night' service, whereby information is available on reservations and vacancies at almost all of the province's main hotels and motels. Local telephone directories provide telephone numbers for these and various other establishments.

Main Newspaper

Telegraph-Journal

Useful Addresses

Tourist Office

Tourism New Brunswick,
PO Box 12345, Fredericton, New Brunswick, Canada, E3B 5C3.

New Brunswick Hostel Association,
c/o National Office, 333 River Road, Vanier, Ontario, K1L 8H9.

NEWFOUNDLAND (Including Labrador)

Area: 156,185 square miles/404,517 square kilometres
Capital: St. John's

Newfoundland includes the 'Grand Banks', comprising extensive fishing grounds to the south east of the province, where fishing is the main industry. Timber, paper production and processing are also significant features of the economy.

Nature surely takes this part of the world as its main residence, where waters teem with fish of many varied species, including salmon, char and pike; over a dozen species of whales circle the waters of the province; and millions of nesting seabirds dominate the untamed ocean shores. On drier land, Newfoundland is home to the world's largest herd of caribou.

Back to the water though, one can surely imagine no more majestic a sight than the masses of icebergs that, breaking free of their neighbours, float southwards to the warmer waters of the Gulf Stream to melt, other that is than the many that run aground to form spectacular 'mountain' regions along Newfoundland's ocean shores. For Canadian tourist officials, these mountains appearing so suddenly on the scene make for a majesty unsurpassed in the northern hemisphere.

With a population of a low 30,000 inhabiting so vast a wilderness, this is more a place for the lover of wildlife and scenery than for the more gregarious of individuals.

Points of Interest

Information Services

A wide range of booklets and information services are available from tourist offices, providing essential information relating to accommodation, places of interest, travel facilities, guided excursions, road maps, and so on. See 'Useful Addresses' to follow.

Main Newspaper

Telegram

Useful Addresses

Tourist Office

Tourism Department of Development,
PO Box 2016, St John's, Newfoundland, A1C 5R8.

NOVA SCOTIA

Area: 21,425 square miles/55,490 square kilometres
Capital: Halifax

A small maritime province and peninsula extending to some 350 miles, Nova Scotia is almost entirely surrounded by water, and is joined to the mainland by a 17-mile long isthmus at the country's border with New Brunswick.

Nova Scotia has the largest indigenous black population in Canada. Additionally, around 77% of inhabitants are of British descent; another 10% are of French extraction.

Agriculture, iron and steel manufacturing, and fishing are the mainstay of the economy.

Here one finds a way of life uniquely private and secluded, with scenery as dramatic and interesting as anything one is ever likely to come by. In excess of 100 provincial parks provide for the recreational needs of visitors and residents.

Nova Scotia is bordered by over 4,000 miles of coastline, ranging from rugged rockfaces to smooth silver sands. Not surprisingly tourist offices confide that this province is renowned for 'splendid coastal scenery, fascinating marine history, colourful marine culture, and warm hospitable people'.

As is the case for many other provinces, Nova Scotia is home to a blend of people from wide ranging ethnic origins, amongst them refugee black American slaves, Scandinavian and French imigres, and perhaps most dominant of all hoards of English and Scottish Protestants whose way of life is reflected today in British-style villages, shops and markets.

Provincial capital Halifax is the centre of business, education and culture, enjoying also status as major tourist and convention centre.

Points of Interest

Information Services

The tourist offices of the province can supply a wide range of essential information to inquirers. See 'Useful Addresses' for further information.

Main Newspaper

Chronicle-Herald

Useful Addresses

Tourist Office

Nova Scotia Department of Tourism,
5151 Terminal Road, 3rd Floor, Box 456, Halifax, Nova Scotia,
  B3J 2R5.

PRINCE EDWARD ISLAND

Area: 2,184 square miles/5,657 square kilometres
Capital: Charlottetown

Located in the gulf of the St. Lawrence river, in this tiny province most employment is in agriculture, fishing and tourism.

Though Prince Edward Island is perhaps best known for its potato production, for those seeking respite from the hustle and bustle that proves a regular feature of life in most parts of the world, it is probably in this province that the remedy will be forthcoming. The sun shines almost constantly even in the depths of the Canadian winter, brightening the already colourful rich red soil and lush green grasslands of the province. The people of the province are also renowned the world over for their own brand of sincere warmth and unreserved hospitality.

Prince Edward Island sports a truly beautiful national park along with dozens of provincial and private parks.

Points of Interest

Information Services

Tourist offices and Visitor Information Centres are able to provide much essential information of help to tourists. Offices are liberally located around the island; the main branch is detailed under 'Useful Addresses'.

Main Newspaper

Guardian

Useful Addresses

Tourist Office

Prince Edward Island Tourism,
PO Box 940, Charlottetown, Prince Edward Island, Canada, C1A 7M5.

Guide to Major Cities

OTTAWA (National capital)

For many newcomers to Canada's capital city located in the province of Ontario, the first impression is one of a skyline dominated by the green copper roofs of the Parliament Buildings, set against a magnificent backdrop of the Gatineau Park and the Ottawa River.

It is to Queen Victoria we owe the designation of Ottawa as capital city of Canada, albeit she first of all named it 'Bytown'. At that time 'Bytown' was the best known work camp in North America, an area in which lumber entirely dominated the way of life for the inhabitants, who were in the main a hard drinking, hard hitting race of shantymen; overworked, underfed and segregated by colour, in the mad dash to extract and export whatever lumber could be had from the region.

And yet from certainly not the most gracious of beginnings, rose a city so rich in natural splendour, that in 1937 the Capital Region Plan set out to restrict all developments in the city to include only those which would in no way impede, hinder or harm the scenery and untamed beauty of the region. In spring the city lights even further to the beauty of the thousands of tulips sent by the Netherlands, as an annual 'thank you' for Canada's wartime protection of the Dutch Royal Family.

A city of old blending well with the new, here we find two modern masterpieces of architecture, the Canadian Museum of Civilization and the National Gallery of Canada, opened in 1988 and 1989 respectively. Two further sites of cultural interest followed, in the shape of the National Aviation Museum and the Canada Museum of Caricature, with plans no doubt in the offing for the Museum of Contemporary Photography opening in the spring of 1992, to be followed by a host of other museums for which the city of Ottawa is renowned.

Those keen on a more active way of life, one that brings them to activities more associated with life in the 1990s, might find their needs well met in the host of recreational facilities provided in and around the city: water rafting, cycling, hiking, swimming, sailing, skiing and hang-gliding, and this names but a few.

Shopping and facilities for eating out in the capital are excellent. Ottawa boasts three excellent multi-national shopping centres: Sparks Street Mall, The Rideau Center and Byward Market.

The city features regularly on the average family's itinerary for holiday venue, coming as one of the few parts of Canada or the United States in which big city life can be enjoyed amongst a mass of wide open spaces and immaculate scenic waterways. Lakes, rivers, parks and the 120 kilometres long Rideau Canal, the latter of which links the city with Lake Ontario, complete the unspoilt beauty of Ottawa.

Amongst the most desirable neighbourhoods in Ottawa, or indeed in the whole of Canada, is Island Park, a sprawling complex of tree-lined avenues sheltering the magnificent and spacious luxury homes of Ottawa's prominent and wealthiest of citizens.

Useful Addresses

A wealth of tourist information is available from tourist offices dotted around the city. Much useful information is also available from:

National Arts Center,
18 Byward Market Street, Ottawa.

TORONTO

Capital city of Ontario, during the late 18th century Toronto was a fortified harbour situated a respectable distance from the American border. Today, Toronto is Canada's largest city, and centre of commerce and finance – 'Bay Street' is to Canadians what 'Wall Street' is to their neighbours a little further south. The CN Tower with glowing spear-like peak, dominates Toronto's skyline at a height of 1815 feet, making it the world's largest free-standing structure.

Located on the northern shores of Lake Ontario, Toronto offers a fascinating combination of modern architecture co-existing with the far quieter tree-lined sectors of the city, which complete with Victorian buildings and a much slower pace of life give every indication of having been transported back to a time more in keeping with that Victorian Britons might well have proved accustomed.

In seeking to attract migrants of all nationalities and cultures, and subsequently encouraging them to retain as much of their ethnic traditions and culture as possible, Toronto has created for itself a multicultural society almost certainly unequalled in any other part of the country.

Torontonians though, do not consider their city a 'melting pot', but a 'salad bowl', the distinction being that though all sub-groups blend in well together, one can still distinguish the unique and individual components of the overall social structure. Here one finds communities of Italian, Chinese, Portuguese and German communities living in close harmony to one another, yet each remaining loyal to its own ethnic origins. In Toronto, the United Church of Canada even conducts services in Korean and Hungarian, amongst a host of other languages; the visitor can watch soccer played Greek style, or else keep an eye on the world as viewed by the Armenian national press.

Just outside of the city one can take a walk back in history to observe a civilisation for whom time seems literally to have stood still for centuries. The religious order of Mennonites, in their tall hats, bonnets and austere black attire, are descended from immigrant German settlers. But instead of blending in well with life in the big city or twentieth century for that matter, devotees still drive around in horse and buggies, and produce a range of cuisine unchanged from that of their ancestors.

Toronto is noted not only for its cleanliness but for a very low crime rate too. As in Ottawa, the old has blended in well with the new, and here one can enjoy the charm and character of early downtown Toronto before venturing back to the glossy facade of the city's newer parts, where one finds that cultured, exciting and affluent atmosphere for which the city is renowned.

Toronto is famed not only for an excellent quality of cuisine, but also for that wide range of ethnic dishes for which its restaurants have achieved worldwide acclaim. Culture too features highly in Toronto's plans for its citizens and visitors alike. Here one finds the headquarters of the National Ballet of Canada; the city is home to its own Symphony Orchestra, and a wide range of excellent theatres, many of them located at the O'Keefe Centre where entertainment is as ethnically varied as those citizens for whom this beautiful city is home.

Those tempted to opt for life in Toronto take warning, for along with not too distant Montreal, this is one of the most expensive places of the world in which to live.

Useful Addresses

Toronto Convention and Tourist Bureau,
Easton Center, Suite 110, Box 510, 220 Yonge Street, Toronto, M5B 2H1.
This tourist office publishes a vast selection of information leaflets and booklets for the visitor and newcomer.
An 'Accommodations Guide' lists all hotels, motels, resorts and fly-in camps in the province of Ontario.

MONTREAL

Largest city in the province of Quebec and often mistaken as its capital, 1992 will find Montreal the scene of much celebration and activity, for this year marks the 350th anniversary of its founding.

Montreal is described by Canadian tourist offices as 'an island with a mountain at its heart', and further as 'three cities in one'. The latter definition stems from the existence of an elegant older part of the city, the new city and centre of commerce and finance, and finally Montreal's underground city. An odd spectacle for those of us more acquainted with life above ground, here one find a multi-level mass of shops, restaurants, cinemas and various other facilities aimed at protecting residents and visitors from the often very harsh winters and sweltering hot summers experienced in the world above.

This, the second largest French-speaking city in the world, the home of 'Quebecois', and lovingly termed 'The Paris of North America'. Not so lovingly however, Montreal ranks with Toronto as one of the most expensive of Canadian or worldwide cities in which to set up home.

Useful Addresses

Tourist Information Centre,
174 rue Notre-Dame East, Montreal.

Maison du Tourisme,
2 Place Ville Marie, Montreal.

QUEBEC CITY

Capital city of the province of Quebec, this is the only walled city north of Mexico (the city once stood as a fortress protecting its citizens from the then hostile world outside). Quebec City stands on a cliff some 860 feet above the St. Lawrence River, offering magnificent panoramic views from almost all parts. Doubtless such featured highly in UNESCO's 1985 declaration of Quebec City as a World Heritage Treasure.

A feeling of almost having stumbled on a clone of France is not surprising, considering that French is the predominant language of 95% of residents.

Useful Addresses

Tourisme Quebec,
Case Postale 20000, Quebec City, Canada GIK 7X2.

VANCOUVER

As largest city in British Columbia, Vancouver is often mistakenly considered capital city of the province.

For sheer beauty Vancouver is difficult – some would suggest impossible – to surpass. Downtown Vancouver with its magnificent display of sky-scrapers, is surrounded on all sides by water. The ocean and a superb panoramic mountain range are observable from almost any point in the city. Parks exist in great abundance, paramount amongst them Stanley Park, covering an area of 1,000 acres and featuring sports facilities, an open-air theatre, a zoo, and an aquarium. Totem poles, nature trails and a miniature railway add to the attraction of this, one of Canada's most magnificent parks.

Vancouver is the financial and cultural heartland of the west coast, a city noted not just for its ability to blend in well with the hustle and bustle of that which is required of such centres of activity, but which can also provide extensive parks and wide open spaces but a few minutes walking distance away. But, even in a city loaded with financial and commercial institutions, life in Vancouver takes on a decidedly laid-back atmosphere, with people happy to enjoy their environment, even if that means escaping a little from the money-chasing scramble that proves so significant a feature of many major cities.

Beauty in the visual sense is not all that greets the visitor to Vancouver, who might be surprised to find a myriad of ethnic restaurants and eating places confronting him in the form of cuisine with origins ranging from Cantonese to Mandarin, Korean, Japanese, Indian, Portuguese, Italian, Greek, Danish, Swiss, British, French, German and Mexican.

Paramount amongst the many desirable neighbourhoods of Vancouver is Dunbar, where a wealth of lush green vegetation, and easy access to beautiful golden beaches, does much to compliment a magnificent range of homes most definitely reserved for the more affluent sections of society.

Useful Addresses

Vancouver Travel Infocenter,
562 Burrard Street, Vancouver.

VICTORIA

The quiet pace of life one encounters in this city belies its status as capital city of the province of British Columbia, a fact that has no doubt contributed to the popular misconception that Vancouver is actually capital.

Victoria is located on Vancouver Island, and portrays an image very close to that one might more likely have expected to find in the streets of Victorian England. Indeed many regard this as the most 'British' of Canadian cities, one which has retained most of its colonial heritage. Perhaps its most majestic sight though, is that of Craigdarroch Castle, a monument built in 1885 by a multi-millionaire coal baron.

Slightly to the north of Victoria lies the Saanich Peninsular, where one finds Butchart Gardens, acres and acres of land given over to a year-long display of brightly coloured blooms.

Useful Addresses

Visitor Information Centre,
812 Wharf Street, Victoria.

FREDERICTON

Capital city of New Brunswick, a magnificent display of elm trees awaits the visitor to this beautiful city located on the banks of the Saint John River.

'Majestic' though is not a word to describe just the scenery, for this city was in fact named in honour of the second son of King George III, and was at one time an important military centre, as can be evidenced by the Officers' Square and Compound from which one can still hear military commands during the changing of the guard, a colourful daily downtown tourist attraction.

Another tourist attraction comes in the form of the first cathedral founded on British soil since the Norman Conquest of 1066, namely Christ Church Cathedral consecrated in 1853.

Useful Addresses

Tourism New Brunswick,
PO Box 12345, Fredericton, New Brunswick, Canada, E3B 5C3.

Further Information

The best source of material by which to familiarise oneself with the various regions is that available from Canadian Tourist boards in Britain and Canada. The London address is:

Canadian Tourist Office,
Canada House, Trafalagar Square, London, SW1Y 5BJ. 071 930 8540

One of the most up-to-date sources of information, which the Canadian High Commission itself recommends to those interested in their country is 'Canada News', available monthly from specified tourist offices, addresses for which are available from the publishers, or else on subscription from the publishers:

Outbound Newspapers,
1 Commercial Road, Eastbourne, East Sussex, BN21 3XQ. 0323 412 001

Maps for most parts of Canada are available in various specialist retailers located in Britain. See 'Yellow Pages' for details. From within Canada, maps are available from:

Gulliver's Travel Bookshop,
609 Bloor Street W, Toronto, Ontario, M6G 1K5.

Oxbow Books,
Box 244 Clarkson, Mississauga, Ontario, L5J 3Y1.

Books of interest, many of them updated annually, include the following:

The Alaska-Yukon Handbook. Publisher: Moon
The Canadian Rockies Trail Guide. Publisher: Bradt
Rocky Mountain National Park Hiking Trails. Publisher: Bradt
Berlitz Guide to Montreal

Fodor's Guide to Canada

Fodor's Guide to Toronto

Fodor's Budget Travel Canada

Fodor's Area Guides
  Canada's Maritime Provinces
  Quebec

Dollarwise Guide to Canada. Publisher: Frommer

Dollarwise Guide to Montreal and Quebec City. Publisher: Frommer

Insight Guide to Canada. Publisher: APA Publications Ltd.

Michelin Green Guide to Canada

Penguin Guide to Canada

CHAPTER TWO

Entry and Residence Regulations

General Advice

That ever open door Canada once made available to migrants from all parts of the world, is now closing rapidly as the unemployment rate amongst its own nationals causes continued concern to the authorities. Gone also to a great degree are those days when Canada relied on skills, education and training imported from outside sources.

Canada as one of the most advanced nations of the world, one in which educational facilities are enviably high, can now adopt that more selective stance as have the governments of Australia and New Zealand.

As a measure of the heavy immigration levels Canada has provided for in recent years, in 1985 immigration approval was allowed to just over 84,000 persons; a year later that figure had risen to almost 100,000, and in 1987 over 115,000 newcomers were permitted entry. Canada today seeks what officials term a 'moderate and controlled increase', one that takes first and foremost the country's needs into account. An estimated one-third of applicants allowed entry are those with relatives resident in the country who are willing to sponsor their entry.

Specific skills and educational qualifications now govern application for permanent entry of independent hopefuls.

Application for entry for whatever purpose and duration is subject to government control, as are applications for employment and residence. Canadian bureaucracy however, though rigid in the enforcement of its rules and regulations, is not renowned for any unnecessary use of red tape or incidence of bureaucratic bungling. Even application for permanent entry to Canada is usually a speedy process and an efficient one at that.

The usual rule is that one must have a job already lined up before entering Canada for the purposes of employment, and work permits will almost certainly be granted only where the prospective employer can adequately prove that no national or landed immigrant is available to carry out the work concerned. It is an offence incidentally, for the visitor to Canada to enter the country with the specific intention of looking for work, other than in the case of those granted status as landed immigrants.

Visas and Passports

British and Commonwealth nationals do not require visas to enter as tourists. A full 10-year passport with six months validity is however required. Those entering as tourists will normally be granted a stay of 90 days, longer if the applicant obtains prior permission from Canadian government representatives in their home country. Passport applications can be made through British post offices and should be sent with the appropriate fee, photographs and supporting documentation to your regional passport office, details of which are available in 'Yellow Pages' or through the services of direct enquiries.

Short Stays

British visitors to Canada do not require visas for stays of up to three months. Those wishing to obtain advance approval for a stay of longer than three months, should contact the **Canadian High Commission (Immigration Department), MacDonald House, 38 Grosvenor Street, London, W1X OAA. 071 409 2071.**

Application for an extended stay made from within Canada must be processed by the appropriate immigration authorities within the country.

Those entering the country for an extended period may need to prove sufficient resources for their financial upkeep whilst in Canada. Additionally, entrants are frequently required to show proof of return travel documentation or sufficient funds to provide for the same.

Residence Permits

Those Britons with valid visas, passports and where appropriate employment authorisation, have right of abode in Canada.

Those intending to work in Canada, without necessarily applying for immigrant status, must first of all obtain Employment Authorisation (form 1102), valid for five months, and covering a previously arranged job offer. The authorisation is not transferable between jobs should one find alternative employment whilst in Canada. Applications for employment authorisations are made to the Canadian High Commission in London.

Those wishing to enter for employment of unspecified duration and to allow for transfer between jobs, might obtain an indeterminate Employment Authorisation, following application to the Canadian High Commission, where as always stringent rules will be applied to ensure that the applicant in question is one who will add to the economy and well-being of Canada and its citizens, and will not be likely to take employment away from nationals or landed immigrants.

Alternatively, students fitting certain criteria might obtain extended job authorisations through:

BUNAC,
16 Bowling Green Lane, London, EC1R OBD.

Conditions are applied to the granting of extended authorisations and those covering unspecified job opportunities, details of which are available from either of the above sources.

Consular Matters

As for those entering whatever other country, the Briton should register with his or her nearest national High Commission or Consulate in the province or territory in which he or she is currently residing.

Officials will then be able to assist with emergency matters whether emanating from within Canada or Britain, and will also be able to offer much useful advice concerning matters regarding passports, residence permits, and many legal and domestic difficulties the Briton might find him or herself encountering.

Addresses of main British High Commission offices and Consulates are listed at the end of this chapter.

Emigrating to Canada

Emigration, known to the Canadians as 'permanent residence', no longer operates on an open door basis. Today, if attempting entry on an independent basis, one must obtain a requisite number of 'points', before there is any chance whatsoever of gaining permanent entry to Canada.

Rising unemployment has stemmed the incoming tide of immigrants, who must, unless qualifying on certain other factors, possess certain skills and qualifications for which the present population is unable to cater. The Canadian authorities in Britain frequently publish a complete and comprehensive list of skills currently in demand. This list is printed regularly in:

'Canada News', obtainable from many travel agencies, or on subscription from:

Outbound Newspapers,
1 Commercial Road, Eastbourne, East Sussex, BN21 3XQ.

A free copy of 'Canada News' is also available from:

Canada House, Trafalgar Square, London.

Note – it is a credit to the editor and publishers of 'Canada News' that, whilst Canadian government representatives in London stress that the publication is private and possesses no links with the Government of Canada, it is accepted as the most comprehensive periodical available in the UK that deals exclusively with Canada.

Special Note

Despite problems of unemployment in many parts of the country, Canadian government officials still envisage that the current immigration level of something in the region of 200,000 per annum, will extend by 1995 to an estimated one-quarter of a million each year.

There are generally two methods of entry for intending independent migrants:

– By obtaining work from a Canadian employer in advance of application for entry. It is the responsibility of the prospective employer to make application on the would-be worker's behalf, something usually accomplished by approaches made to local employment centres where the employer will need to prove justification for offering the position concerned to a non-national.

– By applying for an immigration visa, usually with a job offer received in advance of such application.

Basically, application is made on 'dependent' or 'independent' status, in the first instance where one has relatives already resident in Canada, who might in addition sponsor one's own entry into the country. Those seeking entry as independents usually have no close relatives living in Canada, or at least none prepared to act as sponsor, in which case suitability for entry is estimated by means of a 'points' system, the latter of which takes into account various personal and job-related characteristics.

Information received from the Immigration Section of the Canadian High Commission in London, states that the Canadian government is able to offer two services for people contemplating emigration to Canada. For those who have come to a positive decision and who are willing to pay for the service, there is the option of having the formal application process begin immediately. For those either less determined, or else wary of their chances of acceptance for migrant status, the authorities will carry out a free, no obligation assessment of suitability for entry to Canada.

Government representatives advise those applying as dependants of persons already resident in Canada, that is spouse, dependent child, fiance(e), or parent, to make immediate application. A call to 071 409 2071 will, it is said, will immediately provide inquirers with correct documentation.

Those applying on a self-employed or business footing, in the latter case whether as investor or entrepreneur, should telephone the number given in the last paragraph for their documentation, although in this class the individual will be required to pay a non-refundable processing fee, which at the time of writing is $500.

Intending immigrants with a firm offer of employment that has been approved by Canadian Employment Centres, are also required to contact the same telephone number for their particular batch of instructions and documentation, and will again be required to pay a non-refundable processing fee of $350.

Those applying as independent applicants currently need 70 points or more to qualify for entry. Those points are obtained as a result of assessment of several factors:

- Education
- Knowledge of English and/or French
- Age

- Area of Destination
- Occupational Training
- Occupational Demand
- Occupational Experience
- Arranged Employment
- Personal Assessment

Canadian immigration authorities, whilst recommending immediate application for processing of documentation, on the basis that points currently available might be lost should demand for your particular qualifications and experience diminish, state that points rarely change significantly within a period of six months.

But, if for no reason other than to illustrate that the demand for any particular job can in fact change significantly, at one time television announcers were accorded 10 points towards that level required for admission to Canada; today they get a big fat zero.

The Points Table

A points table applied to 'independent' entrants, issued and updated on a regular basis by the Government of Canada, allocates a number between 1 and 10 to a long, long list of jobs and professional occupations. From this list one can identify his or her present or prospective employment, alongside which a number of '1' will indicate the chances of independent entry on grounds of occupational status are minimal; whilst those beside which a '10' is indicated might consider themselves 'well on the way' already. The list is provided regularly in 'Canada News' and is available from Canadian Immigration representatives in Britain. To illustrate job requirements at the time of entry, the following points were granted in an up-to-date list of mid-1992.

Accountants, auditors and other financial officers	1
Personnel Officers	1
Quantity Surveyors	1
Aerospace Engineers	1
Social Workers and Various Welfare Occupations	5
Probation Officers	5
Half-Way House Supervisors	5
Legal/Medical/Technical Secretaries	5
Audiologists	10
Occupational Therapists	10
Chefs and Cooks – wide range of specialties	10
Blacksmiths	10
Remedial Gymnasts	10

Points are not awarded purely in respect of job potential as we have already considered, but depend too upon all of those factors listed earlier. The highest number of points one can score in respect of all factors combined is 100; the number required to qualify for entry on independent status is 70.

Points are awarded for all manner of factors; at the time of writing those with a relative in Canada, who undertakes to assist the applicant by means of declaring such to the Canadian Immigration Centre in Canada, will be awarded between 10 and 15 points, depending upon the relationship concerned.

At the time of writing, occupations in welfare and community services rank highly on the points scale.

Those claiming entry as business persons and entrepreneurs are awarded 45 points upon qualification.

'Canada News' advises those interested in migrating to contact:

The Immigration Division,
Canadian High Commission, MacDonald House, 38 Grosvenor
Street, London, W1. 071 409 2071

'C.N.' further advises that a telephone call placed just after mid-day is more likely to get through promptly. Actual processing of applications, from presenting one's form to final acceptance, takes between four and six months.

Special Note
Quebec does not have an occupational selection list upon which to assess suitability or otherwise for entry. Consequently, those failing on the strength of employment and professional qualifications to reach that magical figure of 70 points required for entry to other provinces, might find themselves welcomed with open arms to Quebec.

The Application Procedure
As already stated, the application procedure begins with a letter, telephone call or personal visit to the Canadian High Commission immigration department.

The form one is likely to receive as a result of this initial enquiry is headed 'Immigration Questionnaire', in which one is required to provide certain basic information: name, marital status, number of dependent children and so on. Over and above this basic personal information one must produce information regarding intended occupation in Canada; spouse's present or intended occupation; and requires too some indication of the applicant's proficiency in English and/or French.

A few weeks later the applicant is likely to receive some indication as to whether he or she meets the initial selection criteria. If the applicant does not meet the criteria involved, then alternative avenues might be open which will most likely be detailed in the letter received. Sometimes, the applicant is informed quite bluntly that there is no chance of meeting the selection criteria by whatever method of entry one adopts.

For those who do meet initial selection criteria, it is usually suggested that a firm job offer, one acceptable to immigration authorities, might now be sought, or else one might instead seek an undertaking of assistance from a relative already resident in Canada. Now the applicant receives a more lengthy form than that already completed, this time requiring more in-depth information about family, work experience and other biographical details. At this point applicants are informed of the processing fee of $350 which must be paid if the application is to proceed beyond this point. The fee incidentally is non-returnable even if one's application is subsequently turned down.

Usually a month after this form is returned, the applicant is invited to attend for a personal interview with immigration officials. Interviews usually last between 30 and 45 minutes, during which time motivation, attitudes, initiative and other personal and psychological attributes will be assessed by those conducting the interview. This is not a one-sided interview, and the applicant is allowed sufficient time to raise points and questions that concern him or her at this stage.

Those who pass this stage are then passed through for medical examination, along with spouse and any children of married applicants. The examination itself will cost the applicant approximately £95 for each medical carried out.

Successful passing of the medical examination brings a visa for entry to Canada as a landed immigrant. This document is valid for one year after issue.

Work Permits

Work permits, known to Canadians as 'employment authorisations', are required for all forms of employment; application is made to the Canadian Immigration Office.

Authorisation, as is the case for most other parts of the world, is usually granted only where no qualified Canadian or landed immigrant is currently available to carry out the job in question. All jobs, and consequently work permits, must be applied for from outside of Canada; in fact it is an offence to enter the country with the specific purpose of looking for employment.

Details regarding the application of Employment Authorisation for the normal 5 month or an extended period, are provided earlier under 'Residence Permits'.

Usually a work permit might be given for a period of up to 12 months, and at the discretion of immigration authorities, permits for up to three years are often provided for members of senior managerial and executive professions.

Those wishing to enter the country for the purposes of a working holiday will find much useful information available from the Canadian High Commission in London. Request their booklets and information sheets, 'Do You Want to Visit Canada? and 'Do You Want to Work Temporarily in Canada?'

Illegal Working

As stated earlier, all jobs applications must be made from outside of the country. It is an offence to enter Canada with the specific purpose of searching for employment. Those who find employment whilst in the country for tourist or other purposes, must have their prospective employer make application to immigration authorities in the normal way, which might involve application being made only when the intended employee has returned to his or her own country.

High unemployment rates and high levels of immigration, eventually led to a 'Canada-only' employment policy. Strict measures were introduced to control the entry of foreign workers, backed up by rigidly enforced rules, regulations and applications procedures.

The penalty for illegal working, that is without proper government authority, is frequently one of immediate deportation. And yet it still can not be denied that many Britons and other non-nationals do occupy jobs in Canada without proper authorisation, many of them continuing the pretence for many years.

One's chances of discovery quite naturally are greatly increased where one takes up relatively high profile forms of employment: bar tending, door-to-door selling, employment in shops in central locations, and so on. Those occupying high profile jobs without proper authorisation might find discovery leads to a penalty of a more psychological variety, in that it is not uncommon for immigration authorities to raid the workplace in order to reach their prey.

Amongst the less likely candidates for immediate discovery, namely those engaged in relatively low-profile activities, include such as nannies, telephone sales representatives, domestic workers and to a lesser degree sales assistants and helpers in small neighbourhood shops.

That distinction between high and low profile activities however, is not one intended to guide the intending illegal worker in his or her job search. 'Illegal' in Canada, means just that; penalties are harsh; treatment will not be softened to any extent by Canada's affiliation with the British; in short don't do it!

Finally

All countries employ rules and regulations governing entry and residence by non-nationals. For all seeking entry to Canada for whatever duration or reason, information regarding eligibility and various rules and regulations with which one should comply, should be obtained in advance from the Canadian High Commission in London.

Useful Addresses

The Canadian High Commission,
Canada House, Trafalgar Square, London, SW1Y 5BJ. 071 409 2071

Canadian Immigration Division,
MacDonald House, 38 Grosvenor Street, London, W1X OAA. 071 409 2071

Tourism Canada,
Canada House, Trafalgar Square, London, SW1Y 5BJ. 071 930 8540

British High Commissions and Consulates in Canada

British High Commission,
80 Elgin Street, Ottawa, K1P 5K7.

Edmonton
10025 Jasper Avenue, Suite 1404, Edmonton, Alberta T5J 1S6.

Vancouver
111 Melville Street, Suite 800, Vancouver, British Columbia, V6E 3VS.

Toronto
777 Bay Street, Suite 1910, College Park, Toronto, Ontario, M5G 2G2.

Montreal
1155 University Street, Suite 901, Montreal, Quebec, H3B 3A7.

Halifax
1959 Upper Water Street, Suite 1501, Halifax, Nova Scotia, B3J 2X1.

St John's
34 Glencoe Drive, PO Box 8833, St. John's, Newfoundland, A1B 3T2.

CHAPTER THREE

Your Home in Canada

General Advice

That decision to live and work abroad is one that should be made only with full consideration of the type and quality of living accommodation available for your family and yourself. That decision should also take into account not only the needs of the person who will be earning the family's income in the new country, but those who might be left at home during the day; their requirements in terms of comfortable living quarters, access to local amenities such as shops and schools, availability of suitable transport facilities, and such, should also be taken into full consideration.

Several options are available to that person moving to Canada for whatever duration is involved. The person with or without family members, might choose to live with relatives whilst looking for suitable accommodation of their own. If relatives are not available or else living with them presents difficulties of whatever type. The option might instead be one of taking temporary accommodation in hotels, boarding establishments, or else renting accommodation from private or business sources.

Where that decision to live and work in Canada has been made and the individual and family, perhaps from having already experienced life in that country, decide that there is little if any chance of seeking repatriation, the decision might instead be one of making arrangements in advance for suitable rented or purchased accommodation. Such arrangements can be made entirely from outside of the country, though it is perhaps not wise to commit oneself to a lengthy lease or costly mortgage in respect of a property that as yet remains nothing but a picture in a real estate agent's brochure.

Of course that house-hunting expedition to Canada is not the easy or relatively inexpensive option it might be if deciding to move home from Britain to such as nearby France or Germany. Canada's distance and sheer size make for long and costly visits for the purposes of seeking out suitable accommodation, particularly that intended for purchase, adding further to the usual recommendation of government authorities and expatriate advisory services to instead consider the option of temporary accommodation with relatives or taking whatever other temporary accommodation is available.

On a more practical note, Canada, though not presenting much by way of housing and accommodation problems, offers very little low-cost housing, a problem which assumes great importance for immigrants, who are further advised by Immigration authorities to have accommodation pre-arranged where at all possible.

Rents vary widely between and inside provinces, and sometimes one finds the rental asked for one house differs greatly to that for an almost identical building just a few hundred yards away.

Though accommodation often comes as part and parcel of casual and temporary employment in Canada, it very rarely features in full-time permanent employment packages.

Temporary Accommodation

Not surprisingly, given the varying population densities of individual regions and territories, proximity or otherwise to major towns and cities, amenities – or lack of them – what temporary accommodation is available is likely to differ greatly in terms of type, quality and of course cost.

All provincial and territorial tourist offices publish annual guides to facilities and services available in their locality. An invaluable source of information, these guides usually list every conceivable source of accommodation for visitors, workers and residents.

Details of tourist offices are given under the 'City by City, Region by Region' section of Chapter one of 'Live and Work in Canada'.

Again, given the sheer enormity of the country itself, and the range of temporary accommodation available throughout, in this section we can but highlight the main types of accommodation available.

Hotels

Hotel accommodation in all well-populated areas is of the highest standard. Those in outlying areas are also of high standard, though they might come with a little less in the way of luxury facilities than do those in major towns and cities.

In all parts, hotels are available to suit most budgets; whether the visitor or landed immigrant seeks luxurious accommodation in one of the country's top hotels, where he or she might find swimming pools, sauna facilities, and elegant restaurants come as part and parcel of the cost of accommodation, or where instead the visitor is content with the more spartan facilities available in inexpensive hotels that often double as bars and clubs.

All tourist offices are able to provide details and some telephone helplines relating to accommodation services and vacancies available in their areas. Additionally, in Toronto 'Accommodation Toronto', located at 34 Ross Street, provides a free service on behalf of the Hotel Association of Metro Toronto.

Hotels in French-speaking quarters are usually called 'maisons de tourisme' or tourist lodges. Here accommodation tends to be a little less expensive than in the major English-speaking centres of Canada.

In stylish Vancouver, accommodation comes in a great many forms, from up-market luxurious hotels, to hostels, guest houses, even facilities to live in the romantic, peaceful solitude of the many houseboats available for rent.

As for all provinces, tourist and accommodation literature is available from tourist board offices. In Vancouver's case, type, quality, address, price and amenities relating to almost all known accommodations are available in tourist information.

Still in Vancouver, hotels range from the sumptuous and just as costly luxury type, to the cheap but still relatively comfortable variety available in Chinatown. In some parts of Vancouver, that peaceful quiet beauty for which the city is renowned, is spoilt by a wide variety of thankfully inexpensive establishments, best avoided, and even by way of compliment, 'sleazy' seems the most fair and accurate description of their worth.

For those a little more discerning in their choice of accommodation in Vancouver, details of availability and reservation facilities are obtainable from:

The Greater Vancouver Convention Bureau,
Royal Centre, 1600 – 1055 West Georgia, Vancouver.

Tourist Homes and Guest Houses

Much smaller and less luxurious than their hotel counterparts, these forms of accommodation might however present a more relaxed and family atmosphere to the visitor. They will almost certainly come with a far lower price tag than will accommodation offered in hotels of all but the lowest standard.

Again, it's the local tourist office to which one should head for details and addresses of such accommodation available in their area.

Bed and breakfast facilities are also widely available, if not also a little of a drain on one's finances. Tourist offices again keep a register of suitable accommodation and usually will be able to assist with ascertaining where and what vacancies are available before one begins that long and arduous trek between establishments, only to be faced with a long list of 'No Vacancies' signs.

In Toronto the **'Bed and Breakfast Registry',** from which one will obtain similar though often more specific information than that available at tourist offices, is located at 72 Lowther Avenue.

In Montreal a Bed and Breakfast Registry, named **'Montrealers at Home',** provides details of services, prices and accommodation available. 'Bed and Breakfast' services can be dialled direct on 738 9410, or by consulting tourist offices for appropriate information.

In British Columbia a publication entitled **'Town and Country Bed and Breakfast in BC',** provides details of all suitable establishments in Vancouver and the remainder of the province.

In many areas, bed and breakfast facilities are available with farming families. 'Yellow Pages' and tourist offices will provide details of registers available, and sometimes can offer specific details regarding individual establishments.

Motels

Many drive-in motels offer respite to the motorist tiring from long stretches on Canadian highways. For obvious reasons, motels are not usually centrally located; they offer more by way of convenience en route than somewhere to live for long periods at a time. They do not usually come very much less expensive than do hotels and guest houses – as we said, it's the convenience you pay for.

In Toronto, a central information service provides for those interested in motel accommodation. Details are as follows:

The Greater Toronto Motel Association,
2733 Kingston Road, Scarborough, Toronto.

Most towns and cities maintain details of motels in the vicinity, details again available from tourist offices.

Youth Hostels

In most hostels, standard overnight charges are levied. Opening times vary from one region to the next, with urban hostels normally remaining open until midnight or later. Some though, as for their counterparts in many rural areas, close between 10 pm and the early hours of dawn.

Youth hostel accommodation is available to everyone, irrespective of age. British visitors to Canada can take out membership in the UK before travelling abroad.

Details regarding youth hostelling in Toronto may be obtained from:

The Toronto International Youth Hostel,
223 Church Street, Toronto.

The province of Quebec is particularly rich in facilities for hostellers. Montreal's hostels are so 'luxurious' by normal standards, that arriving without a booking is not likely to find you a bed for the night. Montreal's main hostel is located at 3541 rue Aylmer, Milton, Montreal.

Useful Addresses

Canadian Youth Hostelling Association,
(National Office), 1600 James Naismith Drive, Suite 608, Gloucester, Ontario, K1B 5N4. Tel: 613 748 5638. Fax: 613 748 5750

and

Canadian Hostelling Association,
35 River Road, Tower A-3, Vanier, Ontario, KIL 8H9.

Youth Hostel Association,
84 Highgate West Hill, London, N6 6LU.

International Network Hostel,
1263 Hornby, Vancouver.

CHA Ontario Region,
18 Byward Market, Ottawa, Ontario, K1N 7AJ.

Great Lakes Hostelling Association,
217 Church Street, Toronto, Ontario, M58 1Y7.

CHA Saskatchewan Region,
628 Henderson Drive, Regina, Sasketchewan, S4N 5X3.

CHA Yukon,
1600 James Naismith Drive, Gloucester, Ontario, K1B 5N4.

CHA British Columbia Region,
1515 Discovery Street, Vancouver, British Columbia, V6R 4K5.

CHA Manitoba Region,
Manitoba Sports Federation, 1495 St. Matthews, Winnipeg, Manitoba, R3G 3L3.

CHA Southern Alberta Hostelling Association,
203-1414 Kensington Road, Calgary, Alberta, T2N 3P9.

CHA Northern Alberta District,
10926 88th Avenue, Edmonton, Alberta, T6G OZ1.

Local and provincial tourist offices located in most major towns and cities, are available to provide details of youth hostel facilities in their area.

Home Exchange

Home exchange between nationals of Canada and other countries of the world is a very popular option for those seeking short-term accommodation, or accommodation of a predetermined period. Sometimes a car and boat are included in the exchange. A registration fee is usually asked for your home to be added to a register which is then published and usually forwarded to interested parties.

Amongst firms known to provide such services are:

Home Base Holidays,
7 Park Avenue, London, N13 5PG. 081 886 8752

Home Exchange Limited,
8 Hillside High Street, Farningham, Kent, DA4 ODD. 0322 864527

Homelink International,
84 Lees Gardens, Maidenhead, Berkshire, SL6 4NT. 0628 31951

The Independent Traveller,
Dinneford Spring, Thorverton, Exeter, EX5 5NU.

Home Exchange Club,
13 Knightsbridge Green, London, SW1X 7QL.

Intervac,
6 Siddals Lane, Allestree, Derby, DE3 2DY. 0332 558931

How Do Canadians Live?

Standards of Accommodation

Canadians enjoy a high standard of living, and accommodation features prominently in their plans for retaining and maintaining that high standard. There are however regional variations in standards of accommodation, not surprisingly given the size of Canada and its wide range of towns and cities, geographical regions, climatic conditions, population density, and so on.

As is the case for all parts of the world, accommodation of temporary or permanent type is more varied and more costly in major centres and heavy tourist areas.

Of the nationals themselves, more than half of families live in detached homes, many with gardens. Most homes are serviced by oil or natural gas furnaces or electrical heaters.

Furnishings and utilities are not greatly different to those with which we are familiar in Britain. One major difference however is that many Canadians pay direct to maintenance and cleaning contractors for the upkeep of areas around their homes. Where those homes are part of such as an apartment block or similar complex, that management fee might also take into account a charge for caretakers' services, security services, and a charge for cleaning and general maintenance of that shared property.

Canadians on the whole tend to be extremely houseproud, none more so than in the province of Quebec, where statistics show a far higher consumption of household cleaning products than in any other part of the world!

Types of Property

Those titles we give to types of accommodation in Britain differ greatly to those accorded to their Canadian counterparts. The following is a brief definition of accommodation types based on average properties.

- Standard Condominium Apartment – a two-bedroomed apartment, complete with living room and dining room (sometimes combined), kitchen and bathroom. The essential distinguishing feature of this type of property is its location in a high-rise building, each apartment coming complete with a small balcony and underground car parking space.

- Luxury Condominium Apartment – very much similar to the standard alternative, but with greater floor space and usually with the inclusion of a family den, larger balcony and perhaps increased laundry and storage space.

- Standard Townhouse – much like the British row of terraced houses, and usually coming complete with three bedrooms, living room and dining room (sometimes combined), kitchen and bathroom. A garage and basement area are usually included.

- Detached Bungalow – three-bedroom single-storey dwelling with usual range of living areas. Often there is a full basement area included but not usually a den.

- Standard Two-Storey – usually a three-bedroomed, two-storey home with detached garage. Usually has a full basement but does not usually include recreational rooms. This type usually comes detached or semi-detached. Semi-detached properties are often referred to as 'half duplex'.

- Executive Detached Two-Storey – detached two-storey, four-bedroom, with two or more bathrooms, main living room, basement and attached two-car garage.

Prices and Values

An official survey conducted in 1992, showed the following average house prices in Canada's major cities.

Vancouver	$226,110
Victoria	$173,763
Calgary	$132,851
Edmonton	$108,338
Regina	$73,791
Saskatoon	$74,280
Winnipeg	$84,005
Hamilton	$159,322
Ottawa	$146,719
Toronto	$238,501
Windsor	$106,546
Montreal	$117,852
Quebec City	$92,828
Saint John	$80,960
Halifax	$101,199
St. John's	$97,017

Buying Property

Buying property is an expensive business, one that usually requires two incomes to cater for house prices which more than tripled between 1972 and 1987. Usually purchase requires a deposit of between 10 and 25% of basic price; the balance spread over 20 to 30 years.

Research has shown however that ownership of real estate constitutes a very good investment indeed particularly over the long term. In Calgary for instance, a home purchased for the sum of $23,000 in 1971 had seen its value increase a decade later to $108,000, and another decade later in 1991 that house would cost you something in the region of $128,000.

Before that vital decision as to whether to buy or rent property is taken, the migrant should of course establish that this will be a permanent, or at least a long-term move. This and various other factors determine one's decision as to whether to purchase property, paramount amongst those decisions being that of job security and of course expected levels of remuneration. Amongst other highly appropriate factors that should influence one's decision as to what type of house to purchase, and in what neighbourhood, should be included such as: size, type and quality of accommodation; proximity to place of work; availability and standard of neighbourhood facilities, including such as shops, schools, hospitals and public transport services.

A National Housing Act, alongside various other assisted purchase schemes, might come to the intending home owners' rescue. Through federal and provincial assistance, purchasers might gain government-backed mortgages for periods of up to 25 years, subject to certain conditions being complied with. The size of such mortgages as for many things Canadian, varies dramatically from one province to the next.

How to Find Property to Purchase

As is so often the case in Britain, the home hunter normally begins his or her search with a thorough survey of newspapers and freesheets published in the neighbourhood of their intended destination. That perusal of advertisements will no doubt be supplemented by personal visits (where feasible) to real estate agencies either based in the area, or to their branch offices in other parts of the country.

How to Buy Property

Buying property in Canada is not the long drawn out and complicated matter as that usually facing home buyers in Britain. Britons might wait months for their keys to finally be handed over and mortgage details arranged. Not so in Canada, where deals can often be finalised within two weeks of one deciding which property to make one's home.

Estate agents (in Canada known as 'Real Estate Agents'), do however score higher in the percentage profits stakes than do their British counterparts; the latter of whom charge between 1 and 2 per cent of purchase price in comparison to the Real Estate Agents' 5 or 6 per cent.

Laws relating to property purchase tend on the whole to be more complicated than Britain's, with often many varied options available to the purchaser in respect of types of mortgage, repayment periods and so on. The prospective purchaser is therefore advised to consult a specialist real estate lawyer to guide them through the maze of alternatives available.

Canadian Mortgages

The process of purchasing property in Canada takes on a very similar procedure to that with which home owners in Britain are familiar. Familiar terms apply to the transaction: the resultant loan is a 'mortgage'; the 'mortgagee' is the lender of money and the borrower is the 'mortgagor'.

Various types of mortgage exist, each involving differing deposit levels, interest repayment rates, repayment terms, varying periods for renegotiation, insurance premiums, and so on.

Down payments (deposits), normally amount to 10 per cent of the sale price of a predetermined maximum level. In 1991 that maximum property price level for which the 10 per cent down payment applied was set at $180,000. Deposit rates increase proportionately thereafter.

That 90 per cent loan is subject to an insurance premium of up to 2½ per cent of the amount borrowed. The premium itself is added to the monthly amount one makes to repay the original amount of the loan. This insurance premium does not incidentally apply where one makes a down payment of at least 25 per cent of the property's purchase price.

Repayment periods normally extend over 25 years, although many buyers prefer to reduce their repayment period to between 15 and 20 years.

Interest rates are usually fixed for a predetermined period, usually ranging from six months to five years, at the end of which term the mortgage interest rate is renegotiated to that prevailing at the current time.

Capital gains taxes do not apply to profits from the sale of principal residences.

But it isn't just to income levels and potential job security that a decision as to whether or not a loan will be granted will fall. Credit worthiness, length of time in one's present occupation, size of deposit, age and various other factors are also taken into account. One major lender recommends that applicants should ideally have a credit history of at least one year in Canada before confidently expecting a loan to be granted. This particular source recommends that newcomers establish a credit connection early in their move to Canada, perhaps involving such as a bank loan, or purchase of a vehicle on monthly instalments.

Renting Property

The Decision to Rent

At the time of writing, there is something of a glut of apartments available for rent, the problem it seems stemming almost entirely from high unemployment and rising interest rates.

Even when such problems are resolved there is every likelihood that the prospective home hunter will have very little difficulty in finding ample choice of rented accommodation, though high rental charges might present a very real problem indeed. Perhaps not surprisingly, in major towns and cities, rents can prove high to the point of exorbitant, a fact that might well demand that one either earns to a suitably high level, or that two working members will contribute to rental charges.

That decision as to whether to buy or rent one's home is one best made after that all-important first few months have been spent in one's new homeland, when of course it will become far more clearer as to whether or not the transition is likely to be permanent.

Paramount amongst those factors that must be taken into account before looking for suitable accommodation are included the following:

- What type and size of accommodation do I/we require?

- How long do I/we expect to remain in this particular accommodation?

- How much do I want or need to pay?

- Will the accommodation be furnished, and if so, what facilities must be made for one's own household effects, if any? Can furniture and such be kept in storage for an indeterminate period until such time as a move to unfurnished rented accommodation is made or else the decision is made to purchase property? How much will storage cost?

- Can I keep pets in rented accommodation?

- Is the accommodation close to public amenities, shopping facilities and suitable schooling for my/our children?

- What standard of neighbourhood is involved?

Where to Find Property to Rent

One's search for suitable accommodation to rent, might begin with a study of newspapers and freesheets published in the neighbourhood in which one intends to live. Most real estate agents, in addition to selling properties, maintain a register of property available for rent. Many such firms have branch offices in various parts of Canada, thereby alleviating the need to pay a personal call to the city or town concerned.

Rental agencies operate in most major centres, where facilities are available to peruse notice and bulletin boards at one's leisure. Many such agencies, along with local information and tourist agencies provide rental guides and listings of property available.

Renting – The Basics

Those opting for rented property, will usually be asked to sign a lease; a rental agreement usually containing clauses relating to responsibilities and conditions of payment.

Leasing periods normally range from six to twelve months, though there are often facilities for month to month rental. At the onset, you will normally be required to pay a security deposit, usually equal to one month's rent, along with the amount of the first month's rent. Rents are almost universally paid one month in advance.

Renting property involves various charges not always anticipated by those familiar with renting of private or public accommodation in Britain. You might for instance be required to pay an advance sum for electricity, heating and various other consumables. You will also almost certainly be required to take out 'contents' insurance where the property comes as already furnished.

Most rented accommodation comes complete with fridge, cooker, carpets and curtains (or blinds). In some instances, dishwashers, washers and driers also form an integral part of the rental package.

It is important to remember that when renting such as a detached home with garden or yard, there is usually an agreement built into the lease that the occupant will adequately maintain these outside areas. Where rental of a townhouse (terraced house) is involved, upkeep of outside areas is often the responsibility of a specialist management company.

Renting – The Costs

To rent an apartment in Toronto or Vancouver involves fees significantly higher than almost any other part of the country. The lowest rents are usually those of Quebec, Saskatchewan and New Brunswick, where vacancy rates are also amongst the country's highest.

Looking for Property

In many cities, one finds branches of Canada's Mortgage and Housing Corporation, where help and advice is readily available to those seeking to purchase or rent accommodation.

Real Estate Agents and specialist accommodation firms, accommodation registration agencies, and a whole host of property search services operate in all major cities. All major services are listed in Canadian telephone directories and 'Yellow Pages'.

But, as divulged by many British expatriates and migrants to Canada, that search for suitable accommodation for themselves and their families, has often been well serviced by means of placing 'accommodation wanted' advertisements in regional newspapers, freesheets, and even shop windows.

Insurance

Whether one decides to purchase or instead to rent accommodation, insurance will doubtless feature as part of the payment package. Normally cost of house and whatever contents, furnishings, and such, will determine the amount of one's premium.

An obvious point perhaps given that most Britons already accept the necessity for adequate protection against all eventualities, particularly those of the not so inviting nature, insurance of one's home is of primary importance. Usually the occupant will be required to take out a fully comprehensive policy against all conceivable forms of disaster, and in the case of rented furnished accommodation, household fixtures, fittings and furnishings must also be insured against fire, theft, damage, and usually the very same things against which we seek to protect our interests when taking out insurance in Britain.

Fittings and Furnishings

The composition of Canadian homes is not too dissimilar to that with which we are familiar in Britain; comprising kitchen, bathroom, living room and a varying number of bedrooms. Cupboards, closets, plumbing and lighting units are usually built into the structure of the building.

Types of accommodation comes in all shapes and sizes, from the palatial homes of the better parts of major cities, to the small town houses of outlying areas. The number of bedrooms varies proportionately, with some homes having but one bedroom for intended occupation by the retired or bachelor community. Starter homes such as we are familiar with in Britain might offer an additional bedroom to provide for the likelihood of additions to the family.

Living and dining rooms again are similar to those of Britain; sometimes they are separate, sometimes living and dining facilities are provided together in one room.

We could continue this comparison between British and Canadian homes at some length, but perhaps to little effect, for the Briton will as we have said, find very little difference between the styles of living between both countries, at least as far as heavily populated and tourist areas are concerned.

In outlying areas and in such as the Yukon and Northwest territories, many homes are exceedingly spartan by comparison, as often are farm houses in prairie and agricultural regions.

Directory

What follows is but a very, very brief selection of real estate and property specialists. The vast majority of suitable services will be listed in Canada's telephone directories and 'Yellow Pages'.

Kevin Clark,
Re/Max Langden Real Estate, 123 Oakerside Road S.W., Calgary, Alberta, Canada, T2V 4HS. Tel: 0101 403 251 1718. Fax: 0101 403 251 6160
This firm deals in the selling and renting of homes in Western Canada, as well as providing a range of services relating to investments, mortgages and other housing and accommodation matters.

Re/Max Maple Ridge Realty,
22374 Lougheed Hwy, Maple Ridge, British Columbia, Canada, V2X 2T5. Tel: 0101 604 463 4151. Fax: 0101 604 463 6790
Real estate agency with wide network of offices throughout Canada.

21 Qualicum Realty Ltd.,
Box 1180, 113 West 2nd Avenue, Qualicum Beach, British Columbia, Canada, VOR 2TO. Tel: 0101 604 752 9284. Fax: 0101 604 752 2400
Real estate agents providing services in most parts, primarily on Vancouver Island.

Making the Move

Once that decision to leave Britain for Canada has been made, comes the consideration of exactly what to take with you. Are you for instance, going to sell your present home and contents in their entirety and take but a few small precious possessions with you to Canada, as might indeed be the case where that move is one of intended permanent duration?

Will you instead opt to take all but the most unimportant of household and personal items with you, in which case your costs of removal might be quite high? Will you instead decide in favour of a middle of the road approach and take certain items with you, perhaps just lighter personal possessions, in which case you will then furnish your home anew once established in Canada?

And what of the family car? Will that feature significantly in your removals plans, given that driving in Canada takes place on the opposite side of the road to that on which Britons drive at home? Is it worth taking the car with you considering the costs of removal? Is it worth having your present car transported to Canada, then converted ready for easier and more appropriate use to the rules of the road in Canada?

Moving home, whether to an area near to your present residence or to a land many thousands of miles away, ranks highly in the most distressing of factors facing the individual; one known to cause serious symptoms of both physical and mental illness.

And yet, given a little time, consideration and a careful analysis of the many professional advisors and services available to help with your relocation, often undertaking that transaction down to the minutest detail, there is very little reason that moving whatever furniture, household and personal effects, even pets, to Canada, should present any trouble whatsoever to the intending migrant.

What worries face individuals in their choice of removals expert? As for removals close to home, there is the possibility of careless hands causing damage, or worse still losing pieces of high financial or irreplaceable items of sentimental value. Will your possessions ever reach your new home when required, or will they instead be held up somewhere on route, maybe for long periods of time? Will your goods and household effects reach their intended destination at all?

Who will supervise the packing and unpacking of your goods; who will monitor their progress as they journey from your present home to that of their intended delivery? Does the firm concerned realise that painting is a valuable work of art, and not something your child 'knocked out' during last year's summer holidays? Does that firm indeed care one iota about that painting, or glassware, sculptures, ornaments ...?

With apologies for having planted potential doubts and fears into the minds of intending migrants to Canada, it must be stressed that there is very little reason to expect that your goods and chattels will not be treated with the greatest regard, and this is a situation you can virtually guarantee by choosing your removal agents with the utmost care. Paramount amongst those considerations that should assist in making a suitable and reliable choice are such as ensuring that your chosen firm has membership of an appropriate professional organisation such as the British Association of Removers Overseas or the Association of International Removers.

Other professional bodies include the Household Goods Forwarders' Association of America Inc.

Other factors to be taken into account before making that final decision are whether or not the company will provide a free quotation for their services, one they are prepared to commit to writing; whether the firm itself provides skilled packers and whether packing will take place in your home, where you can at least keep a close eye on the treatment delivered to your precious possessions; whether the company offers door-to-door and fully inclusive insurance cover; and finally does the company provide any personal protection in the event it should cease trading?

And amongst the little-known details that professional exporting removals firms will be able to advise the customer on, include the fact that VAT is usually reclaimable on items purchased within the six months intended for export to another country; all that VAT authorities usually require is some proof of purchase and intention to export. Choosing a 'user-friendly' removals firm could well save you a great deal more than that current 17 per cent VAT refund on whatever might be purchased for use in one's new homeland.

Removals Firms, Packing and Shipping Agents

The Pantechnicon,
Unit 3, 5 The Gate Centre, Sion Gateway, Great West Road,
   Brentford, Middlesex, W8 9DD. 081 568 6195
Branches also in Ascot, Birmingham, Cardiff, Cwmbran, Lincoln and Stourbridge.

Neale and Wilkinson Ltd.,
Freepost, London, SE15 2BR. 071 277 7410
Specialist removers of suitcases, cars, part loads, complete home effects.

Davies Turner,
Overseas House, Stewarts Road, London, SW8 4UG. 071 622
   4393
Specialist removers of entire home contents, part loads, etc.

Blatchpack,
Lodge Trading Estate, Broadclyst, Exeter, Devon, EX5 3EA.
   0392 61721
Branch also at Bristol – 0272 665996
Specialist removers of full and part container loads, household furniture and effects, baggage and cars.

George Copsey and Co Ltd.,
Danes Road, Romford, Essex, London, RM7 OHL.
   Freephone: 0800 289 658
Specialist removers of full and part container loads, household effects, furniture and baggage.

Pets

For specific information regarding taking one's family pet or pets to Canada, including details of several firms able to undertake the transportation for you, please refer to that section 'Pets' in Chapter 5 'Living in Canada'.

CHAPTER FOUR

Finding a Job in Canada

General Advice

Unless retiring to Canada, or else entering as an entrepreneur or investor, the individual will almost certainly be required to find suitable employment to support him or herself and family, as well as to qualify for residence permits.

Some jobs are obtained entirely from within the UK without the individual necessarily being required to visit Canada at any stage in the job hunting process. This is the case where such as representatives of Canadian recruitment and staff placement firms visit Britain to interview potential recruits, or where recruitment is left entirely to a firm or organisation operating exclusively in Britain.

At other times, the job hunter will be required to visit Canada, whether for the purpose of interview, to attend suitable training courses, induction and probationary training or whatever, before that job is finally acquired.

The services of Canadian Manpower Centres are available for the use of landed immigrants. Vacancies are displayed in some 400 centres located throughout Canada, appropriate addresses are available through Canadian High Commissions.

As would be the case for seeking alternative employment in one's homeland, there are a number of questions the intending migrant should ask him or herself before making any decision concerning work in Canada.

Primary amongst those considerations are:

- Is the job permanent or temporary? Will I have to satisfactorily complete a probationary period?
- What hours of work are involved? What wage will I receive? How is that wage made up? Are any bonus, overtime, unsocial hours payments included?
- What deductions are made from my gross wage?
- Do I get sickness payments? What conditions must I comply with regarding sickness leave?

The Demand for Foreign Staff

Canada's present level of unemployment stands at an average of close to 10%.

A wide variety of seasonal and casual opportunities are available to working holidaymakers and short-term contracted employees in Canada. Most such opportunities come with all accommodation and sometimes travel costs included as part of the employment package.

Those intending to make this their new homeland are not however faced with a similarly open range of alternatives; Canada no longer requires the same number or quality of immigrants who once featured so heavily in her 'open door' immigration policy that led to a heavy influx of unqualified migrants from virtually all parts of the world.

A mature country, one highly respected in the sectors of industry, business and commerce, a country able to provide more than adequately for the training of nationals to fill whatever jobs and professional positions fall vacant, Canada can now afford to be highly selective of those persons permitted permanent residence within her boundaries.

As the section on immigration points out, there are in general two methods of entry to Canada; on dependent status namely where relatives are available within Canada's resident population and who will in turn sponsor your entry to the country; and secondly as independent migrants, whose entry is determined by business, investment and qualifications factors, with suitability for entry being subject to assessment in terms of an applied points system.

The points system of course relies almost entirely, other than for business and entrepreneurial classes, upon the qualifications and skills one has to offer for which indigenous supply is currently inadequate. At the present time there is a very high demand for professional health care, welfare and community services employees.

And in many parts, much to the unfortunate disgust of Canadian domestic workers, there exists an on-going and strong demand for British nannies, live-in housekeepers, chauffeurs, butlers, and full-time gardeners, most such opportunities existing in the province of Quebec.

Pay and Working Conditions

A recent study by New York-based Backer Spielvogel Bates indicates that Canadian workers are amongst the happiest and most contented of worldwide employees. The analysis suggests that Canadian companies tend to operate closer links with their workforces, which in turn rewards them with a greater degree of employee loyalty, and in many cases leads to low labour turnover rates and fewer strikes than experienced in many other parts of the world.

The Canada Labour (Standards) Code, is the only federal law governing wages, and applies mainly to government employees and those employed in industries with specific federal connections.

This code does however provide for equal pay and prohibits discrimination on grounds of sex, race, colour and religion, as well as forming the basis of provincial laws for all professions and jobs.

Government employees and workers in federal related industries work a five day, 40 hour week. Set payments must be made in respect of all additional working hours up to a maximum of 48 hours, over and above which higher overtime rates must usually be paid.

Paid annual holidays in most occupations vary between two and four weeks, and an additional ten public holidays are nationally recognised.

Canadian industry boasts exemplary safety standards, with many firms striving to supplement those already high standards laid down by law.

Federal law demands that in certain industries, primarily those in the construction field, health and safety representatives must be chosen from amongst the workforce, and the minister of labour may order the establishment of specific health and safety committees in those organisations where hazardous conditions exist.

Approximately one-third of the labour force belongs to trade unions. Collective bargaining systems function under the auspices of the federal Industrial Relations and Disputes Investigation Act; in addition all provinces lay down their own rules and regulations aimed at creating and maintaining harmony and safe, efficient working practises. Canada has an impressive labour relations record; figures issued in 1991 showed that time lost to major strikes equalled a 25-year low, standing at around 5 days for every 10,000 man shifts worked.

Certain key workers are forbidden to strike, notably those in fire and police services, hospital administration, where the life, health or safety of others might be endangered by a refusal to work.

Though opportunities are available in all provinces, albeit to a varying degree, the greatest level of industrial and commercial employees are concentrated into the province of Ontario. Ontario has an Employment Standards Act in force, by which to lay down those rules governing working hours, minimum wages, public holidays, overtime and holiday payments, and rules relating to equal pay for equal work.

In Ontario, normal hours of work must not exceed 8 hours a day or 48 hours a week. A minimum wage of the equivalent of £3 an hour applies and employees are entitled to 8 public holidays a year. With the completion of 12 months employment, the employer becomes entitled to 2 weeks holiday pay, or an amount equal to at least 4% of the total wages for the year to which the holiday entitlement relates. Equal rights require that females are not paid less than males for work of equal value, unless payment is reduced by factors other than sex.

Health and safety of work is provided for by the Occupational Health and Safety Act, wherein is spelled out those responsibilities falling to all employers and employees, in order to reduce accident levels and encourage higher standards of health and safety for all. Though the majority of responsibility falls to the employer, the job of ensuring a safe working environment must be one carried out by means of sharing information with the workforce, via health and safety representation and joint employer/employee health and safety committee meeting and working practices.

In 1990 an act was passed to restrict workplace smoking. The Smoking in the Workplace Act requires that employers either designate a particular area for smoking or else ban it altogether.

The Employment Standards Act

Included amongst the protection measures provided under this particular piece of legislation are the following:

- Working hours – normally must not be more than eight hours a day, six days a week, or a total of 48 hours a week.

- With certain exceptions, hours in excess of 44 per week must be paid at one and an half times the normal hourly rate.

- Those who qualify for public holidays are entitled to 7 statutory days with pay. Boxing day incidentally, is not a recognised statutory holiday.

- After one year working for the same employer, the individual is entitled to at least two weeks' paid holiday leave.

- All employers must provide written wage statements detailing rate, deductions, living allowances and net pay.

- Equal pay for equal work – employers are not allowed to pay men and women different rates for similar work, unless due to a factor other than sex.

- Maternity leave – women employed by the same employer for at least 12 months, at 11 weeks before expected date of delivery, are entitled to 17 weeks unpaid maternity leave. Women who cease to work on the grounds of pregnancy may apply for benefits under the Unemployment Insurance Maternity scheme.

- Periods of Notice – Those employed for more than three months must receive notice as follows:
  - One week's notice or payment in lieu thereof for periods of employment ranging from three months to two years.
  - Two weeks' notice or pay for periods of employment between two and five years.
  - Four weeks' notice or pay in lieu for periods of employment lasting between five and ten years.
  - For periods of employment lasting beyond ten years, eight weeks' notice or payment in lieu thereof is required.

- Minimum employment age – Though children must remain in education until the age of 16 years, parents of children aged 14 and 15 may make application for alternative programmes allowing part-time or full-time employment alongside adequate educational facilities.

Social Insurance Numbers (SIN)

All employees have their own Social Insurance Number, much akin to the National Insurance number with which we are familiar in Britain. This number will feature on sickness, taxation and most other employment administration documents.

You can obtain your SIN from any Canadian Employment Centre, the details for which are listed in the blue pages of all Canadian telephone directories.

Matching Demand and Your Skills

Those seeking employment in Canada, might find their present skills already provide a healthy contribution to the points one must obtain for hope of eventual immigrant status. It might instead be that the applicant needs to obtain new skills and qualifications, perhaps take a refresher course or upgrade those skills he or she acquired some time before. Perhaps the applicant might instead plan for him or herself a course of training that leads specifically towards qualifications for positions featuring high on Canada's skills required tables.

All of these factors and considerations the individual may well be able to plan for without any outside assistance; sometimes this is not the case however, especially where that person is not altogether certain of his or her suitability for training and potential entry to an entirely new career.

As for the many problems life has to throw in our path, a body of experts are there to guide us through the maze of alternative answers to whatever lies at the root of our concerns; in this case it is career analysts to whom the potentially confused Canada-bound hopeful might turn his or her attention.

Career Analysts (sometimes termed 'consultants'), will assess the individual's personal and academic qualifications and abilities for almost any career or job you may care to contemplate. They will advise the applicant for or against potential careers; suggest training and experience options open to them; perhaps recommend institutions available to cater for individual training, educational and works experience needs.

A few such analysts are listed below. This list is by no means exhaustive, and although all reasonable steps are taken throughout 'Live and Work in Canada' to point the reader only in the direction of highly reputable and efficient firms and services, it is the individual's responsibility to ensure that whatever organisation he or she approaches for whatever purpose, is one best suited to his or her needs.

Career Analysts

Career Analysts,
90 Gloucester Place, London, W1H 4BL. 071 935 5452

Chusid Lander Career Counsellors Ltd.,
35-37 Fitzroy Street, London, W1P 5AF. 071 580 6771

Independent Assessment and Research Centre,
17 Portland Place, London, W1N 3AF. 071 935 2373

Career Development Centre for Women,
97 Mallard Place, Twickenham, Middlesex, TW1 4SW. 081 892 3806

In addition, even the most highly qualified individual might in many instances find him or herself required to register with the appropriate Canadian body for the profession of which he or she is a member. Where appropriate contact the Canadian equivalent of your professional organisation in order to ascertain whatever procedure is involved to allow you to transfer your professional skills to that country.

Special Note

The intending migrant is advised not to pin his or her hopes of entry to Canada on the obtaining of qualifications relating to a job or employment opportunity currently ranking high on the scale of points accorded to independent applicants.

This advice applies particularly where a long and arduous course of study is required to obtain that end qualification, since although such is a rare occurrence, it is not unknown for a job or profession once ranking highly on the points table to shortly fail to score even one miserly point for its hard-working and hopelessly disillusioned practitioner.

It is essential therefore, that those entering into a career in whatever sector, and whatever length of training is involved, should undergo such training with qualification as their primary and overriding objective; transfer of their skills to Canada, albeit paramount amongst one's personal expectations should be assigned a back seat role.

Qualifications

As we have said on many occasions in 'Live and Work in Canada', even those with the highest of British academic and professional qualifications might find their credentials subject to scrutiny by Canadian professional bodies before they are allowed to occupy positions of anywhere near the level they enjoyed in Britain. More often than not this is little more than a formality which involves contacting the appropriate Canadian professional body, to which details of one's qualifications will be forwarded for consideration of suitability for employment in Canada.

Nevertheless, it is still likely that the migrant may be required to serve a probationary period in his or her new position, perhaps even enter the profession he or she has been a member of for many years, at a much lower rung on the professional ladder. As always, if something is worth having, despite the inevitable blow to one's morale, that 'something' is undoubtedly worth working – an also worth waiting for.

Sources of Jobs

Assuming that you have already decided upon the type of position or job you intend to seek, including the intended duration of such employment, you must of course now decide exactly how to go about obtaining information regarding vacancies and analysing methods of applying for whatever openings are available.

Fortunately, despite the fact that the job hunter is many thousands of miles removed from his or her prospective place of future employment, there are a great number of methods available by which to gain access to appropriate vacancies in Canada.

Most of these methods will be considered in the following sections, though one must not of course forget the fact that a number of other options exist, including such as word of mouth from persons to have recently visited Canada for whatever purpose; information available from those who have already returned from a working tour of duty in that country; people – and they are in the minority – who have decided on repatriation to Britain when migration proves not to live up to their earlier expectations.

One expatriate service able to put intending migrants in touch with people already to have experienced life in Canada, including not only those who have opted for repatriation, but also those for whom life in Canada has more than fulfilled their earlier hopes and dreams, is the following:

Focus Information Services,
47-49 Gower Street, London, WC1E 6HR. 071 631 4367

Primary amongst the other sources of information available to the intending short-term worker or migrant to Canada, are those which will now be considered in detail.

High Commissions and Consulates

It is not, as the reader will doubtless be aware, a prime function of government representatives abroad, to assist their own or foreign nationals in their search for job vacancies.

Having said this, many embassies and consulates do offer the facilities of their reading rooms to anyone interested in scouring national newspapers for appropriate job advertisements. One will find the Canadian High Commission in London particularly helpful in this respect. Agents-General of the various provinces usually have access to up-to-date details of job vacancies within their respective regions. Addresses for offices in London are as follows:

Alberta
1 Mount Street, London, W1Y 5AA

British Columbia
1 Regent Street, London, SW1Y 4NS

Nova Scotia
14 Pall Mall, London, SW1Y 5LU

Ontario
21 Knightsbridge, London, SW1X 7LY

Quebec
59 Pall Mall, London, SW1 5JH

Saskatchewan
16 Berkeley Street, London, W1X 5AE

Chambers of Commerce

Chambers of Commerce in Britain and Canada, might well prove an excellent source of job vacancies, professional openings, along with providing much useful information regarding opportunities for entrepreneurs, investors and business personnel.

Chambers of Commerce are often able to provide lists of British companies operating from bases in Canada, from which such list the intending job seeker might make personal application to prospective organisations.

Useful Addresses

London Chamber of Commerce,
69 Cannon Street, London, EC4N 5AB. 071 248 4444

Canada/UK Chamber of Commerce,
3 Regent Street, London, SW1Y 4NZ. 071 930 7711

Canadian Chamber of Commerce,
55 Metcalfe Street No. 1160, Ottawa, Ontario, K1P 6N4.

Newspapers

Almost all daily and weekly editions of the national and local press feature some jobs opportunities overseas, as a visit to your local newspaper reference library will no doubt indicate. Foreign newspapers, obviously primarily Canadian publications, also feature significantly in the enthusiastic job hunter's plans. Many larger British newspaper reference libraries maintain a stock of British and foreign newspapers, the most comprehensive being that of:

The London City Business Library,
106 Fenchurch Street, London, EC3M 5JB. 071 638 8215

For obvious reasons the best place in which to look for job openings or else to place 'situations wanted' advertisements is in Canadian newspapers themselves. Such newspapers are available for consultation in the London City Business Library mentioned above, as well as on subscription from agents operating in Britain. See Chapter 5 'Living in Canada' for full details of main provincial newspapers. Though almost all such newspapers carry job vacancy sections, the reader's attention is drawn to two excellent sources of job advertisements. Printed in British Columbia, 'Province' and 'Westender' will greatly assist with the search for jobs in BC and other provinces.

Two excellent directories of worldwide newspapers, magazines and other publications, available in all reference libraries are 'Willing's Press Guide' and 'Benn's Media Directory'.

Additionally, the 'Advertisers' Annual' available again in most reference libraries, is an invaluable source of details relating to major foreign newspapers and periodicals, and their agents in Britain.

Another invaluable aid is the 'Ayer Directory of Publications', in which are listed all Canadian and worldwide newspapers of interest to job hunters.

Amongst major British newspapers known to include a fair selection of foreign job opportunities are included: The Daily Telegraph, Sunday Telegraph, Guardian, Times, Sunday Times, Financial Times, Daily Mail, Daily Express and Independent on Sunday.

Special Note

Please refer to 'Advertising in Newspapers' a little further on in this chapter.

Journals and Magazines

Professional and trades journals and magazines are of course an excellent source of foreign job opportunities. Many such house journals exist, far too numerous to mention in our text, but including: Accountancy, British Medical Journal, Caterer and Hotelkeeper, Computer Weekly, Construction News, The Economist, Nursing Times, and Times Educational Supplement.

Details of most professional journals are available in 'Benn's Media Directory' and 'Willings Press Guide, both of which are available for reference in most libraries. Once you have located the professional publication of your choice, write for a few back copies. Most such bodies are more than happy to provide the information you require, usually with a nominal processing charge being requested for the service.

Specialist Bulletins and Expatriate Briefing Services

Many such services operate either exclusively to keep the intending migrant aware of jobs available in various parts of the world, whilst others offer such information as an adjunct to another role or function. Amongst those services known to provide a jobs update facility are included the following:

Overseas Jobs Express,
PO Box 22, Brighton, BN1 6HX.
Provides a monthly newspaper incorporating articles, advice, tips and information to intending workers abroad, along with details of many current jobs vacancies in all parts of the world.

Overseas Consultants,
PO Box 152, Douglas, Isle of Man.
Offers various services including a fortnightly updating service of opportunities available overseas.

LEADS,
4 Cranley Road, Newbury Park, Ilford, Essex, IG2 6AG.

Offer various services to intending and actual expatriates including details of current job opportunities in most parts of the world.

Jobs Overseas,
Job-Search Publications, PO Box 35, Falmouth, Cornwall, TR11 3UB.
A monthly newsletter providing articles, advice and tips to intending expatriates and workers overseas, along with a large selection of worldwide jobs opportunities.

The Expatriate,
First Market Intelligence Limited, 56a Rochester Row, Westminster, London, SW1P 1JU.
A monthly newsletter packed with articles, features, country profiles, and listings of jobs available overseas.

Expat. Network,
Carolyn House, 5th Floor, Dingwall Road, Croydon, Surrey, CRO 9XF.
Total support service for expatriates and intending expatriates, including monthly publication 'Nexus', in which are outlined jobs available overseas. This company also operates an employment register, and advertises vacancies in 'JOBLINK' circulating members' details to employers overseas. Expat. Network also operate a computer database scheme for urgent matching of employer/employee requirements.

Careers International,
P S Publishing, Speer House, 40 – 44 The Parade, Claygate, Surrey, KT10 9QE.

Graduate Posting,
Newpoint Publishing, St. James's Lane, London, N10 3DF.

Intel Jobs Extract,
Intel, Duke House, 33 Waterloo Street, Hove, Sussex, BN3 1AN.

Special Note
One bulletin providing exclusively for job hunters to Canada is:

Overseas Employment Newsletter,
PO Box 460, Town of Mount Royal, Quebec, Canada, H3P 3C7.

Professional Associations

Most professional bodies operate some form of overseas job hunting facilities for their members. Those known to maintain registers and offer personal briefings services, or else produce professional newsletters containing overseas jobs advertisements are therefore included under appropriate headings, when we come to consider the main job opportunities existing in Canada.

Write asking whether such a service is available, and if not, whether you can instead be provided with details of their corresponding Canadian-based professional bodies.

UK Job Centres

An excellent place to start one's search for employment in Britain, one can also find job centres in Britain and Canada, able to provide details of jobs available in the latter.

It might be unlikely that vacancies will be posted on notice boards for the job hunters' perusal, and usually what is required of the latter is an informal chat with job centre officials, who if they can not provide details of specific job vacancies in Canada, might well be able to place the inquirer in contact with colleagues of job centres or other agencies who can provide more detailed information.

Canadian Job Centres

Landed immigrants are allowed the services of Canadian Manpower Centres, in which are displayed lists of jobs currently available. Some 400 centres operate across the country, addresses for which are available from Canadian High Commissions.

Canadian Employment Centres (CECs) list job vacancies and provide information on exactly how to go about making application for those which might prove of interest. Job training is also available through CECs, thus usually providing an ideal opportunity for the newcomer to Canada to at least obtain some experience of Canadian working practises, as well as affording the employee an opportunity to adapt his or her own skills in line with what is expected by Canadian employers. For many newcomers the answer is to take whatever job presents itself, the objective being one of acquiring work experience upon which to build one's future career in the new homeland.

Private Agencies

Private agencies not unnaturally operate on a fee-paying basis, though not always one which requires an unreasonable outlay when viewed in terms of the invaluable information provided.

Some operate to requirements provided by Canadian employers, from which the agency will subsequently place advertisements in appropriate publications, and provide information to job centres and other recruitment agencies. The intention here is to locate potentially suitable applicants, who will then go forward for shortlisting perhaps by joint consultation between the employment agency and the Canadian employer. Interviews might subsequently be the sole responsibility of the agency, the Canadian employer, or else a combined effort might be involved before job offers are made to successful job applicants.

Other agencies maintain a register of individuals interested in working abroad, from which they will then extract appropriate personal and employment-related data before attempting to search suitable vacancies, details of which might then be passed direct to the job hunter for personal application to be made. The agency might instead pass details of all such individuals to employers with known job and professional vacancies.

Alternatively, the agency might combine both practices, maintaining a register of intending employers and prospective employees, who will then be compared for mutual suitability, interviews set up, or else details passed to the Canadian organisation to undertake all recruitment procedures on its own account.

Canadian Recruitment Agencies

Catering for placements of individuals to all occupations is:

Overseas Employment Services,
PO Box 460, Town of Mt. Royal, Quebec, Canada, H3P 3C7.

One Canadian firm whose representatives visit London monthly for the purposes of conducting initial interviews for intending migrants is:

Brownstein,
Brownstein & Associates of Montreal. 514 939 9559

UK Recruitment Agencies

A wide variety of British agencies are available to locate and notify appropriate vacancies for intending workers in Canada. Access to information relating to the most likely agencies for job hunters' requirements, are available from:

FRES (Federation of Recruitment and Employment Services),
10 Belgrave Square, London, SW1X 8PH.

Specific British-based agencies are detailed under respective job and professional headings when we come to investigate the main opportunities available in Canada.

With compliments

Outbound Newspapers

The Newspaper Group for International Immigration and Tourism

1 COMMERCIAL ROAD, EASTBOURNE, EAST SUSSEX BN21 3XQ

Special Note

Medical, various professional employees, designers and selected industrial workers, are able to find placements by means contact with the following agency:

Transcontinental,
18 High Street, Beckenham, Kent, BR3 1BL. 081 650 2344

Recent advertisements placed by this agency have included vacancies for physiotherapists, occupational therapists, project and production engineers, computer professionals, toolmakers, machinists, motor mechanics, panel beaters, wood machinists and veneerers.

Advertising in Newspapers

Many job vacancies, as we have already considered, are advertised in Canadian newspapers to which the job hunter might have little or no ready access. Many reference libraries hold stocks of Canadian newspapers, as do various offices of the Canadian government operating in Britain.

Where access to newspapers is still not an easy option for the job hunter, he or she might consider approaching press representatives of Canadian publications based in Britain. The 'Advertisers' Annual', as considered earlier, is available in most main reference libraries, and will provide details regarding British agents of Canadian newspapers.

Amongst those known to operate an efficient service are:

Powers Overseas Ltd.,
Duncan House, Duncan Square, London, SW1V 3PS. 071 834 5566
(Agents for the 'Montreal Star' and can assist with placements of jobs advertisements)

Media Universal Services,
34-35 Skylines, Lime Harbour, Docklands, London, E14 9TA. 071 538 5505
(Can assist with subscriptions and placement of advertisements in most worldwide publications)

The really astute job hunter will not however need to restrict his or her activities to seeking out advertisements placed by intending employers. Individuals can take the initiative themselves by placing 'situations wanted' advertisements in Canadian newspapers, either operating direct with the newspaper concerned or with the help of agents.

Writing Letters

Another method of taking the initiative in the search for suitable jobs, is that speculative approach frequently taken by those seeking jobs within Britain, namely by writing to firms and companies to ask whether suitable openings are currently available, or else likely to fall vacant in the future.

Those who have tried this approach will be aware that often many letters have to be written before a positive reply of any sort is forthcoming. The usual response is one of 'thank you – we will keep your name on file'. Though this response is often viewed – sometimes realistically so – as 'fobbing off' persistent job hunters whose chances of obtaining employment with firms concerned verge near a zero rating, there are many organisations which do actually maintain a register of suitable people upon whose services they might call at a moment's notice.

So, given that we must accept the fact that just one organisation willing to place our name and career details on file might be just the stimulus our job hunting expedition requires, to whom can we address those speculative letters? In general, four main opportunities present themselves:

1 Canadian companies operating in the United Kingdom or else have bases or subsidiaries in this country

2 Canadian companies operating exclusively from that country

3 British companies known to operate from bases also in Canada

4 Canadian-based British companies or their subsidiaries

An ideal source of information regarding companies, firms and organisations to contact are international trade directories, copies of which are available in all main reference libraries. At the conclusion of this chapter you will find a brief selection of such companies and appropriate addresses in Britain and Canada.

When writing speculative letters to potential employers, the basic rules of good letter writing are of paramount importance, if you are to create that essentially favourable first impression on someone who has not asked for details regarding you or your suitability for employment with them.

Nothing too fancy is required in sending a polite letter of inquiry to prospective employers. Often a simple letter to indicate you are looking for suitable employment and consequently you take the opportunity to enclose your curriculum vitae for the reader's perusal will usually more than adequately suit your purposes.

The curriculum vitae (CV), today's version of the now antiquated employment application form, can be produced by the job applicant if that person feels capable of creating a professional, concise, but fully comprehensive document, or else it can be produced on your behalf by a proliferation of outside agencies where charges for such services can seem extortionately high, but in fact are well worth the fees involved for a document that will greatly enhance the chance of obtaining employment either for jobs advertised or where instead making inquiries of potentially suitable organisations. We will deal more closely with the production of CVs and letters a little later in this section.

Personal Visits

Those visiting firms and institutes with the intention of seeking out whatever vacancies might be available, should take with them a curriculum vitae (English with French translation where appropriate), along with references and educational certificates, similarly translated into French where required.

But it must be remembered that it is usually illegal to enter Canada with the specific and unauthorised intention of seeking employment, meaning of course that personal visits of this nature are almost entirely ruled out.

Such rules and regulations do not prohibit one from visiting British-based offices of Canadian businesses and other prospective employers, or British firms known also to operate in Canada, or else to have subsidiaries operating in that country. Again access to a trade directory, available in most main reference libraries, will indicate those British addresses to which you might make personal representation.

Chambers of Commerce are also invaluable sources of suitable information for those intending to personally visit firms with which employment in Canada might be sought.

Other useful sources of such information include the many yearbooks available for perusal in reference libraries, included amongst such volumes: 'The Bankers' Almanac and Yearbook', 'The Insurance Directory and Yearbook', 'The Oil and Gas International Yearbook', and many, many others. Chambers of Commerce Yearbooks, though providing much extremely useful information, are not available on all reference library shelves, so make a telephone call to local libraries before turning up out of the blue to obtain access to this particular work or reference.

Further Sources of Useful Information

Addresses of prospective employers in Canada, may be obtained from the following books available for reference in most major reference libraries:

The Canadian Trade Index

The Canadian Almanac and Directory

Most trade unions and professional organisations are able to provide information relating to jobs vacant within their own particular disciplines. Two very useful volumes containing details of such organisations are:

Trade Associations and Professional Bodies in the United Kingdom

Professional Organisations in the Commonwealth

Applying for Jobs – Advice and Tips

Job hunting and subsequent application normally takes place via the medium of the letter of application, application form, or more likely via the curriculum vitae (CV), or 'resume' as the ostentatious CV is better known to the Canadians.

Job advertisements are placed in daily and weekly Canadian newspapers. Those of more menial duties and responsibilities might be placed in factory entrances, in shop and large store windows, in public buildings, employment agencies, union hiring halls, on college bulletin boards, in pharmacies, and if you haven't guessed it by now, in almost all places by which to bring the vacancies concerned to public prominence.

Federal and provincial governments maintain job centres for use by all job hunters, including newcomers. Jobs are displayed in much the same fashion as that with which we are familiar in Britain, and there are also opportunities on display for jobs-skills training either operating along with or separate to full-time employment opportunities.

Immigrants possessing foreign professional and academic qualifications must usually have their qualifications approved by the appropriate authorities in that province in which they intend to work. Canadian Employment Centres will provide all such advice regarding having one's credentials approved, as will the equivalent Canadian organisation for the profession or trade concerned. In some cases, the individual might be required to serve a probationary term, even in a job or profession he or she has carried out for many years in their original homeland.

A recent article in 'Canada News' advises that even the most highly trained of immigrant professionals can find themselves unable to compete on an equal footing with their Canadian counterparts possessing far less in the way of qualifications and experience than themselves. For many, the only option is to accept gratefully a job of far lower status than that one occupied in Britain, from there to begin another climb up the professional ladder.

Job application and interview procedures actually bear very close resemblance to those with which the British job hunter is doubtless familiar, other of course than in the case of those jobs falling vacant in primarily French-speaking sections of the country. Often one might be faced with the dilemma as to whether or not to apply for that job in English or in French. As a general rule, if the job is advertised in English then one should normally make one's application in English; if instead advertised in French, or else if is specified that applications be made in that language, then in the latter case one should of course comply with that request. Where the advertisement is in French but no indication is given as to what language the application should be made in, the applicant might then take the opportunity of making application in both languages.

That applicant for whom French is not a working language whether in conversation or in writing, will find his or her needs met via many translation services available in all parts of Britain, most of them listed under 'Translators and Interpreters' in 'Yellow Pages'.

Letters of Application

Whether to accompany one's curriculum vitae or else to act as a vehicle of application in its own right, the individual should always prepare some form of letter addressed to the prospective employer.

Accuracy, tidiness and attention to detail are essential pre-requisites of letters of application as well as those designed to accompany your curriculum vitae.

Let us consider by way of illustration what goes towards a simple yet concise letter of application:

William B. Smith,
10 Main Street,
Suretown,
London,
AA1 B22,
England

Tel: London 123456

21st April, 19—

J. B. Employer, Esq.,
Certain Industries Plc.,
PO Box 234,
Place Victoria,
Montreal,
Quebec,
H4Z 1J7

Dear Mr ... (Ms./Miss/Mrs or where not certain 'Sirs')

I wish to apply for the position of consultant personnel manager as advertised in the April 1992 edition of 'Going Places'.

I am 27 years of age and currently employed as personnel manager with Miracle Industries, a subsidiary of Major Company Industrial Products based in Enfield, Middlesex.

My duties include the full range of personnel management services, and include total responsibility for recruitment and induction training of shop floor and office staff.

I have held this position for seven years, during which time I successfully studied for the professional qualifications of the Institute of Personnel Management. In addition I have attended several courses at local colleges and universities, most of them in the specialties of recruitment and labour relations.

I speak fluent German and am now studying French by correspondence course.

I am particularly keen to secure employment in Canada, and feel that with the personnel management qualifications and experience I can offer, I might be able to make a contribution to your own company, especially in the light of your job description which I have of course studied in detail.

I trust the above information is sufficient for your requirements and shall be happy to provide any further information you might require.

I look forward to hearing from you in due course.

Yours sincerely,

W B Smith

William B Smith

Special Points

1 Where the letter is speculative, that is one made without knowledge of any suitable vacancies currently existing, the writer should omit the first paragraph and in its place enter:

'I write to enquire as to whether you might currently, or in the near future, have vacancies for ... (position/job/ profession concerned)

2 Where the letter is one made following notification of a suitable vacancy and formal application is requested by presentation of a curriculum vitae, the applicant should instead omit all of the above body text and insert in its place something to the effect:

'I wish to apply for the vacancy of ... as recently advertised in ... and enclose my curriculum vitae for your perusal. I shall be happy to provide any further details you may require and look forward to hearing from you in due course'

3 The writer can, even in a speculative letter of introduction, send his or her curriculum vitae with a short letter of introduction. The letter itself would then become one of simply stating 'I wish to enquire ...', following which the letter will finish with a paragraph to the effect:

'I enclose my curriculum vitae for your perusal and look forward to hearing from you in due course'.

Curriculum Vitae

The curriculum vitae, a relatively modern concept, was designed initially to replace the once universal job application form, which if well designed, actually presented few problems to either applicant or prospective employer.

Most application forms though, were hastily produced and largely incapable of providing for the needs of often thousands of individuals who might be required to complete that particular form during its current print run.

The curriculum vitae, despite its awesome title, is an 'open' document, one the applicant produces him or herself and can therefore confidently produce this vitally important document in relative certainty that all important details have been included. Many firms as we have already discussed will produce a curriculum vitae on the applicant's behalf, many of these firms able to offer an updating service primarily by means of retaining client details on computer disk ready for a speedy and inexpensive update.

Usually all that information required for a comprehensive curriculum vitae falls within three broad categories:

personal

career

educational

To break this down a little further, under those broad headings one would expect to find information included regarding the following sub-sections:

- Personal – name, address, telephone number, nationality, age, date of birth, place of birth, marital status, hobbies, special interests

- Career – present and past employers, dates of employment, positions held, general responsibilities, special responsibilities, courses attended, reason for seeking alternative employment

- Education – schools, colleges and universities attended; courses taken by other means including correspondence, examinations passed with grades attained, various non-academic qualifications

Now let us take a fictitious curriculum vitae to illustrate the basic layout of those details outlined above.

CURRICULUM VITAE

Name:	Mary Jane Harrison
Address:	Rosebank Cottage, The Village, Dawson Town, Surrey, VV1 2DD, England
Telephone:	Dawson Town (3333) 56789
Date of Birth:	2nd April 1970
Place of Birth:	Fulham, London
Age:	21
Nationality:	British
Marital Status:	Single
Education:	Dawson Town Grammar School, The Street, Dawson Town, Surrey, England

Qualifications:	General Certificate of Secondary Education GCSE Ordinary 'O' Level (Seven subjects) French (grade B) English Language (A) Mathematics (B) Physics (B) Geography (A) History (A) Art (C)
Positions of Responsibility:	School head girl Captain of school netball team
Present Position:	Accounts Clerk, City Solicitors, Back Street, Dawson Town, Surrey, England. February 1987 – present date
Reason for Seeking Alternative Employment:	Advancement and desire to live in Canada
Interests and Activities:	Reading, writing poetry, computer programming
Other Information:	Clean driving licence
Referees:	Mr R Walsh, Accounts Manager, City Solicitors, Back Street, Dawson Town, Surrey, England
	Reverend J. Manners, The Parsonage, Neartown, Surrey England

Note

Where applicants have greater work experience, a further heading 'Career history' should be inserted after details relating to present employment and reason for seeking alternative employment. In this case the applicant would then list in reverse chronological order all jobs held together with a brief indication of the responsibilities of each.

For those wishing to prepare their own CV, and remember it isn't a long or difficult proposition to prepare a highly professional document in its entirety, the above basic format will fulfil most requirements.

Special Points

1 Applicants with relevant academic and professional qualifications can send with their letter and/or curriculum vitae photocopies of relevant certificates.

2 Though not held in as high regard as references that might be obtained direct from present and past employers, testimonials presented by past employers to the applicant can similarly be photocopied and sent with letters of application and/or curriculum vitae.

3 Many people have a passport size photograph attached to their curriculum vitae, for the simple purpose of easing that initial meeting between intending employer and prospective employee once that vital interview stage is reached.

Dealing with Interviews

One of the most prohibitive and potentially worrying aspects of preparing oneself for interviews with prospective employers in Canada, is the possibility of long and expensive journeys to wherever the interview will take place. The situation is of course less fraught with problems should that interview be held in the United Kingdom, as is often the case where the Canadian employer passes all responsibility for recruitment to a specialist employment and recruitment agency operating within the United Kingdom.

In most instances, whether interviews are held in the United Kingdom or Canada, interview expenses will either be offered in advance of the interviewee making his or her journey, or else usually where shorter distances are involved the interviewee might be required to claim expenses retrospectively.

The big problem of course, presents itself where no expenses are offered, in which case the applicant must carefully weigh up the chances of obtaining the position concerned, along with his or her motives for seeking employment in Canada in the light of those high costs that will inevitably ensue.

On a more realistic footing it must be stressed that few Canadian employers are going to request that you attend for interview without offering expenses. Given the time and distance involved in making your way to an interview whether held in Canada, or more often in London where that application is made through a British recruitment agency, the prospective employer has already taken great care to ensure that at least on paper, interviewees are more than capable and sufficiently well qualified to carry out the duties of the position involved. Nine out of ten times expenses will be paid.

Where you are required to make your own way to the place of interview and provide for all expenses incurred, make absolutely certain whether or not expenses will subsequently be reimbursed. To reiterate, where you will not be reimbursed, then consider carefully your chances of obtaining the job in the light of costs involved.

As a general rule then, jobs advertised in the United Kingdom will almost certainly have interviews held in this country, usually in London. Those interviews resulting from advertisements placed in the Canadian press or else obtained by means of a speculative approach to Canadian employers will usually have interviews held in Canada, unless that firm also operates from bases in the United Kingdom, in which case interviews might be held closer to home.

Interviews, given Britain's close allegiance with Canada, operate on a very similar basis to the norm for such meetings held in the former country. Today's interviews are not held on anywhere near the formal footing once renowned for greatly increasing the interview nerves of prospective candidates, and informality is usually the order of the day for interviews held in Britain and Canada.

That once one-sided interview in which the prospective employer did much of the talking, leaving that other person sitting at the far end of a long and foreboding desk is gone; in its place is a two-way discussion often conducted on first name terms, obviously with questions asked of the candidate, but always with sufficient time allowed for that person to answer questions in full, and with opportunity also to ask questions in turn of his or her prospective employers.

Many very good books are to be found on the subject of job application and interview techniques, to which the less experienced interviewee should at least refer prior to setting out for that meeting upon which his or her future depends. Most such books are available in lending and public reference libraries, and can be purchased for very little cost from most good book shops.

Language

This is where the greatest problem usually presents itself,

particularly for those applying for job in primarily French-speaking parts of the country. Will the applicant be expected to conduct the interview in French? Is a knowledge of French essential to the job concerned, in which case those applicants without such a knowledge would almost certainly not reach the interview stage in the first place?

For those possessing a working knowledge of French, then fewer problems are likely to exist. In the unlikely event that one encounters an interview invitation to be conducted entirely in French but for a job in which fluency is not a crucial qualification, then if the interview panel does not itself provide for the services of an interpreter, there is every possibility that the applicant will be allowed to engage the services of an interpreter. As always, make sure you cover all eventualities well in advance of making that trip for interview.

Incidentally, even where interviews are conducted in the French language, and the panel is aware that you possess an inadequate knowledge of their language to allow a reasonable exchange of views, information and opinions to take place, a favourable impression will certainly be made should you offer greeting and make your exit with those simple phrases 'Bonjour' (good day, good morning, good afternoon), and 'Merci' (thank you). And should you find yourself not on first name terms with your interviewers then instead of referring to them as 'Mister', 'Miss' or 'Mrs', elect instead for 'Monsieur', 'Mademoiselle' and 'Madame'.

Finally, it is a matter of pure courtesy, but a highly impressive one at that, to subsequently write a note of thanks for being invited to interview.

Accepting a Job Abroad

Though most of the following points are those one would consider when pursuing employment in the United Kingdom, and many of them should in fact be clarified prior to the interview stage, it becomes even more important given distance and costs involved in transferring one's employment to a foreign land, to make absolutely certain the following factors are taken into account and all problems, queries and uncertainties fully ironed out before accepting a job abroad.

One must therefore take into account:

- the suitability in Canada of UK academic and professional qualifications

- how and where to obtain appropriate authorisation to work in Canada
- length of the contract of employment
- what the employment package comprises
- whether travel, housing and other forms of relocation assistance are included in the package
- whether a probationary period is involved
- what wage or salary is paid, how and when
- what deductions are made and how much in involved
- hours of work, overtime rates, holiday entitlement
- housing and proximity to place of work
- what opportunities, if any, exist for advancement
- pension and sickness provisions
- any further requirement before employment will be made permanent, eg training courses, requirement to take courses or study for further qualifications, medical tests, and so on

Contracts and Permits – A Note

One's employment contract will detail much the same matters as included in the last section, and bear close resemblance to their British counterparts. The purpose of a contract is not just to inform that person offered employment of what conditions are attached to the job. It also serves to establish a contractual relationship between employer and employee, one by which to lay down what each might expect of the other, as well as the process by which potential disputes might be resolved.

Periods of notice on either side, disciplinary procedures, labour relations policies, job responsibilities, all feature alongside those factors that form the basic employment package.

In most cases it is the employer in Canada who must apply for necessary work permits or 'employment authorisations'. To avoid unnecessary duplication of facts, the reader is referred to 'Work Permits' and 'Illegal Working' as featured in Chapter two – 'Entry and Residence Regulations'.

Working for a Canadian Employer

Working for a Canadian employer bears great similarity to that of working for a British employer. Very often employees and employers are on first name terms; often they meet outside of the working environment for social purposes.

First name terms again are often the order of the day between working colleagues and employees/employers, facilitating a far more relaxed working environment than exists in many other parts of the world.

As is the case for those working for British employers, disputes and grievances will doubtless sometimes find their way to the ears of union and employee representatives. More usually, and especially where an open relationship exists between employers and employees, that grievance or dispute might instead be communicated quite amicably between both sides of the employee/employer relationship.

Women Working and Living in Canada

Equality of opportunity for women working in Canada is the focus of much concern from women's rights groups, government and many employers. Legislation is however seeking to urgently redress what imbalance does undoubtedly exist in many sectors and more specifically in certain provinces.

In Ontario, stringent new laws require that all women whose jobs compare equally to men's, must have whatever reduced level of wages made up to that level enjoyed by men. Individual companies are required to register their plans and timetables for redressing whatever inequality of wages might exist with respective provincial government departments. Jobs are graded according to several factors, mainly those of skills required, effort exerted, working conditions, and level of responsibility pertaining to the job. Subsequent grades are then compared with those jobs held usually by men.

A recent study conducted by the United Nations showed that in Britain, America and Canada, the average woman's wage is half – sometimes less – that received by men.

As is the case in Britain, a great many more Canadian women, immigrants and nationals alike, now seek to supplement their family income by means of working outside of the home. Between 1951 and 1986, the number of women workers in Quebec rose by 297 per cent. In that province the number of working mothers increased by almost 20% in just five years from 1981 to 1986, reflecting not only a desire on the part of women to re-enter the workforce, but often indicating that a second income is now a virtual necessity for those purchasing their own homes whilst maintaining a reasonable standard of living for themselves and their families.

But in certain sectors of the overall employment market women are encountering great difficulty in gaining entry. A recent survey conducted for the Canadian Education Association for instance, revealed that very few women reach the rank of principal in schools whatever province they work in. In British Columbia it was calculated that only 4 per cent of college or school principals are women; in Alberta the figure stands even lower at one woman principal for every thirty positions, and in no province did that level rise above 12 per cent. In Quebec and Ontario however, women fare far better in the employment stakes, with one in eight and one in ten school and college principals respectively coming from the ranks of females.

Inroads have however been made for women in the business world, where even though just six per cent of directors chairs are filled by women, this figure doubles that which applied just five years before, at least indicating that employment opportunities for women are slowly but surely improving.

Women accompanying their partners to Canada will usually discover it relatively easy to transfer most skills to their new homeland once that decision is taken to enter or re-enter the workforce.

Adult further education courses proliferate in most parts of the country; the woman, or man for that matter, might easily increase his or her academic and professional qualifications and skills from within the country.

As in most countries of the world there are still many professions and occupations that might well be described as female-dominated: hairdressing, nursing, beauty culture, catering and many health care functions being those that spring readily to mind.

Getting Posted to Canada

The Possibilities and Potential

Usually jobs in Canada are applied for direct, though doubtless there will be some opportunity to apply for jobs within the UK with the prime intention of transfer to employment in Canada. The individual faces various options: he or she might choose to apply for employment for a Canadian firm that possesses a base within the United Kingdom; he or she might instead choose to apply for employment with a British employer known to operate also from Canada.

Problems tend on the whole to present themselves where individuals seek employment with British or Canadian employees in the precise hope of transfer or secondment to Canada, something which is a very far from realistic option in all but a minority of cases.

Details of British companies trading within Canada and vice versa, as well as details of companies with strong mutual trading links will usually be available from Chambers of Commerce. Refer to your local 'Yellow Pages' and trade directories in local reference libraries for details of offices from which information might be obtained.

How to Go About It

The first step is to obtain details of British companies with bases in Canada or vice versa, to which application might be made by hopeful Canada-bound individuals. Yet still there will remain a great many job vacancies of which the individual might remain blissfully unaware. Such information might best be obtained by means of access to Canadian newspapers such as might be held for reference purposes in major libraries, or else by taking out subscriptions to any of the many job information bulletins currently available, and widely advertised in the national press.

Application, once that job vacancy comes to the attention of the prospective employee should be processed in whatever manner might be appropriate in Britain. What should not be assumed however, is that obtaining the job in question is a definite passport to a life across the Atlantic.

Finally

We reiterate that general rule applied throughout 'Live and Work in Canada', namely that it is impossible to cover all possibilities regarding access to information relating to job vacancies existing in Canada today or in the future. Very many sources of such information exist, and the reader must be prepared to explore any and every such avenue at his or her disposal, all of course depending on the intended duration and type of employment involved.

Sources of Further Information

'**International Pay and Benefits Survey**', a fully comprehensive guide to what the worker in whatever part of the world might expect from employment in the host country, is available from:

P A Personal Services,
Hyde Park House, 60a Knightsbridge, London, SW1X 7LE.

'**The Executive Cost of Living Survey**', can be obtained through:

Business International,
Human Resources Division, 12 – 14 Chemin Rieu, 1211 Geneva
  17, Switzerland.
and from their British office situated at:
40 Duke Street, London, W1A 1DW.

'**Directory of Canadian Companies Overseas**', is published by:

Overseas Employment Services,
PO Box 460, Town of Mount Royal, Quebec, Canada, H3P 3C7.

'**Directory of Canadian Employment Agencies**', is available from:

Overseas Consultants,
PO Box 152, Douglas, Isle of Man.

The Main Types of Work in Canada

The greatest level of opportunities fall in Ontario, the heartland of Canadian industry and commerce. Ontario in fact boasts the employment of more than 40% of Canada's scientific and engineering professionals, along with 40% of employees possessing qualifications at post-secondary school level.

Women feature prominently in the workforce here, offering employment to over half of Canada's female workers. That British women intending to enter as main 'breadwinner' for the family she takes with her will find her passage in no way impeded by pure fact of gender. Nor will the wife of a male applicant usually encounter any difficulty in finding suitable employment or training facilities, either immediately upon entry to the country or at some appropriate time in the future.

As said so many times before, Canada being so huge a country, with such great diversity of geographical features, cultures, traditions and life styles, the range of jobs carried out are extremely varied, and will doubtless cover very many more careers, jobs and professions than we can give credit for in 'Live and Work in Canada'.

It must also be remembered that entry for independent applicants, namely those intending to spend the remainder of their working lives in Canada, depends upon the possession of particular skills, academic qualifications and experience. Those entering for business or investment purposes are not included in that basic statement incidentally, since their applications for entry are dealt with separately to those for intending migrant workers and professionals. That points system upon which permission or otherwise to enter is primarily based changes from time to time; skills that are in great demand today might not necessarily be placed very high on the points scale a year or so from now. Requirements also vary between provinces, and the intending migrant must therefore be aware that refusal for entry to one province might not carry over to the next.

Those determined to migrate should therefore consider the possibility of making their homes wherever the job and not the fancy takes them. Immigration officials will provide extremely detailed information regarding those jobs, professions, and provinces which lend themselves best to acceptance for entry to Canada.

Those intending to work in Canada for shorter periods, for instance on secondment for a year or so with their present employers who have operations in Canada, as well as those desiring to spend weeks, months or years in the country, will find their needs regarding work and residence permits explained in an earlier chapter 'Entry and Residence Regulations', though again Canadian immigration authorities are ever keen to help with whatever enquiries you might have to make.

Where appropriate working holiday opportunities are detailed under separate sections. See also 'Casual Work' towards the end of this section.

Accountancy, Banking, Finance, Insurance

Canada being so advanced a country, one with many cities and strong trading links with most other countries of the world, there obviously is a thriving financial sector to which those with suitable qualifications might turn their attention.

But again due to Canada's advanced educational system, the country is almost one hundred percent able to supply for her financial sector's staffing needs from within her own population. 'Accountants auditors and other financial officers', therefore score a meagre one point on the occupations list for those seeking permanent entry as independent migrants. This does not mean however that suitable openings will not occur on a reasonably regular basis for temporary staff, sometimes permanent staff, with particular experience gained in another part of the world. Secondment within one's present employing firm is also a real possibility for those currently or hoping to work in the sectors of accountancy, banking, finance and insurance.

Accountancy

One recruitment consultancy specialist known to regularly recruit qualified accountants for employment in various parts of the world is:

Offshore Specialist Appointments,
Tower Hill Steps, 16 Le Brodage, St. Peter Port, Guernsey.

Professional Association

Institute of Chartered Accountants,
PO Box 433, Chartered Accountants' Hall, Moorgate Place,
London, EC2P 2BJ.

Banking

What the majority of people used to banks proliferating in almost every high street bank fail to realise, is that almost all have considerable overseas operations, many of them represented in virtually every part of the world.

Consequently, even though 'banking' as such might not always feature high on the migration points scale, there is always some opportunity for employees of major British banks to eventually find themselves posted abroad, usually by personal request. This does not mean however, that one should enter banking as a newcomer, purely on intention of achieving an overseas posting. But it can not be dismissed as a possibility to those for whom banking features high in their range of preferred careers.

Most of the major high street banks: Lloyds, Barclays, Midland and Natwest, offer placements abroad, usually after the incumbent has served a reliable 'apprenticeship' in Britain. But there also exist a group of banks whose major operations take place overseas. The reader is advised, if that intention to enter banking is one motivated by a desire to live and work in Canada, to consult the following reference books and contact organisations listed below.

Reference:

'International Bankers' Directory', published by:

Financial Publishing Group,
43 Hamilton Street, Chester, CH2 3JQ. 0244 316879

'The Bankers Almanac and Yearbook', available for reference in most major libraries.

Recruitment Agencies

William Channing,
Clarendon House, 11-12 Clifford Street, London, London, W1X
1RB. 071 491 1338

Useful Addresses:

British Overseas and Commonwealth Banks Association,
8 Old Jewry, London, EC2R 8ED. 071 600 0822

Foreign Banks Association,
4 Bishopsgate, London, EC2N 4AD. 071 283 1080

Barclays Plc.,
54 Lombard Street, London, EC3P 3AH. 071 626 1567

Lloyds Bank Plc.,
71 Lombard Street, London, EC3P 3BS. 071 626 1500

Midland Bank Plc.,
Poultry, London, EC2P 2BX. 071 260 8000

National Bank Plc.,
41 Lothbury, London, EC2P 2BP. 071 726 1000

Finance (Including 'Insurance')

Financial services are a rapidly growing sector in all parts of the civilised world. Not surprisingly many financial firms in whatever part of the world they are based, have expanded their enterprises to many other, particularly larger countries.

Those seeking entry to a financial organisation with the specific intention of being posted to Canada, might find themselves competing with several other colleagues with similar intentions. As said on so many other occasions in 'Live and Work in Canada', that decision to pursue a career in finance should be one motivated primarily by a commitment to the job itself, rather than one designed to bring future travel plans to fruition.

Reference

'**Financial Times World Insurance Yearbooks**', published by Longman.

Recruitment Agencies

William Channing,
Clarendon House, 11-12 Clifford Street, London, W1X 1RB. 071 491 1338

Consultancy International Ltd.,
40-41 Pall Mall, London, SW1Y 5JG.

Wrightson Wood Ltd.,
11 Grosvenor Place, London, SW1X 7HH.

Professional Associations

The Institute of Actuaries,
Staple Inn Hall, High Holborn, London, WC1V 7QJ.

Useful Addresses

Commercial Union Assurance Co. Plc.,
St Helens, 1 Undershaft, London, EC3P 3DQ. 071 283 7500

Legal and General Group Plc.,
Temple Court, 11 Queen Victoria Street, London, EC4N 4TP. 071 528 6200

Administrative & Secretarial

Given its wide ranging business, commercial, financial and industrial interests, Canada has many openings for administrative and secretarial staff at all levels. The country's dual language system provides many opportunities for those able to offer bilingual secretarial and administrative skills.

Unfortunately with the exception of specialist secretaries such as medical and legal executives, such skills do not feature high on the points list for those intending to rely on them for immigration to Canada.

Most opportunities advertised in such as 'The Times' and 'The Guardian' tend to have been placed by international organisations and multinational companies.

Those already granted approval to search for employment within Canada, that is as landed immigrants or perhaps the spouse of that person originally to make application for independent status will find many job openings available, ranging from basic filing and clerical work, to higher skilled and executive class secretarial and administrative positions. It must be remembered however, that those living and seeking such employment in French-speaking parts of Canada, will find their chances severely impeded if that 'working' knowledge of the French language is absent from their curriculum vitae or application form.

Recruitment Agencies

Several agencies exist to offer placements of varying duration, included amongst them:

International Association for the Exchange of Students for Technical Experience,
The Central Bureau, Seymour Mews House, Seymour Mews, London, W1H 9PE.

International Secretaries,
174 New Bond Street, London, W1Y 9PT.

Manpower,
Manpower House, 270/272 High Street, Slough, SL1 1LJ.

Overseas Placing Unit,
4th Floor, Steel City House, Moorfoot, Sheffield, S1 4PQ.

Agriculture, Harvesting, Fruit Picking and Farming

A positive wealth of opportunities await those not afraid of a little hard work, long hours and often lucrative wages awaiting them at the end off the working week. Many jobs are available on a seasonal basis, though it is possible to virtually work one's way around Canada's many harvesting areas, consequently availing oneself of long periods of paid employment.

British Columbia presents more opportunities to the seasonal worker, normally extending from the end of March to the End of July. In many cases the work can prove very well paid indeed by normal standards in other parts of the country. What's more, living costs on whatever site one works are usually extremely low, presenting many seasonal workers with an ideal opportunity to save a little cash at the same time as enjoying working and living in some of the most beautiful parts of Canada.

Under the umbrella of 'Agriculture, Harvesting, etc.', one might also include the thriving tobacco industry of Southern Ontario, and the large selection of albeit smaller plantations operating on Prince Edward Island. Harvesting usually takes place between July and September, providing seasonal opportunities for which the work is hard, but wages more than adequate to compensate for whatever strains and pains one's labours might entail.

Within the general agricultural sector, opportunities of varying duration are available via the following:

Canadien National CN France,
1 rue Scribe, Paris, France.

Frontiers Foundation Inc.,
Operation Beaver, 2615 Danforth Avenue, Suite 203, Toronto, Ontario, Canada, M4C 1LS.

International Farm Experience Programme,
YFC Centre, National Agricultural Centre, Kenilworth, Warwickshire, CV8 2LG.

Willing Workers on Organic Farms (Canada),
RR2 Carlson Road, Nelson, British Columbia, Canada, VIL 5P5.

International Agricultural Exchange Associations,
NFYFC Centre, National Agricultural Centre, Kenilworth, Warwicks, CV8 2L9.
Visits of varying duration can be arranged for single people between the ages of 19 and 28, usually with some experience of farming or horticulture being required.

Fruit picking presents many opportunities to the seasonal worker, most of them offered primarily to women who apparently have that more gentle touch upon which the quality of fruit will depend. Amongst the major fruits grown, and consequently in need of harvesting are: cherries, peaches, plums, pears, apricots and apples. The Okanagan Valley of British Columbia presents perhaps the most 'fruitful' range of opportunities to seasonal workers and working holidaymakers. Harvesting time is generally between late June and late October.

A growing wine industry in the Okanagan Valley presents opportunities for grape pickers, usually between September and October.

Local grape and fruit growers associations, listed in Canadian telephone directories, are the best point of contact for opportunities available. Agricultural Employment Service offices located in various regions will also provide information concerning opportunities in their region, but only to those with legal authority to seek work in the first place.

Fruit growing plantations flourish in Ontario, where vegetable harvesting also offers a fairly reliable source of seasonal opportunities to 'legal' applicants. Much useful information is contained in the leaflet 'Seasonal Employment in Ontario', available from any of the 20 plus Agricultural Employment Offices located throughout Ontario. The headquarters of the AES are based at 12 Grote Street, St Catherines, Ontario.

Communications

Under the umbrella of 'communications' we find various specialties including: telecommunications, radio and satellite communications.

In so advanced a country, communications naturally figure significantly in the economy, but Canada is in general able to provide for staffing requirements from within her own population. Consequently, in respect of those involved in installation and maintenance of these systems, ranking comes low on the points system for those seeking migrant entry on independent status – average score is 1.

A higher score is accorded to those with specialist skills in radio and television broadcasting, sound and video recording and reproduction, sound mixing, stereo-tape editing, re-recording mixing, sound effects and so on, most of these occupations scoring towards the middle of the points table, at the time of writing the average score is 5.

Recruitment Agencies

Anders Glaser Wills,
International Personnel Consultants, 134 High Street,
   Southampton, SO1 OBR. 0703 223511

Beechwood Recruitment Ltd.,
221 High Street, London, W3 9BY.

Grange Selection,
1 Jubilee Road, Chelsfield, Orpington, Kent, BR6 7QZ.

Wrightson Wood Ltd.,
11 Grosvenor Place, London, SW1X 7HH.

Computers/Information Technology

A highly industrialised nation, Canada not surprisingly has many openings for such as computer programmers, systems analysts, systems designers and computer engineers.

But, given Canada's excellent educational system, computer programmers do not feature high on the 'points' scale for migrant entry. Most such opportunities as might take the expatriate to

Canada are therefore likely to be of a short-term or specialist nature, or else will be the result of secondment by one's present employer.

Journals and Publications

Computer Weekly, Computer Talk, Computing, Electronics Express, Freelance Informer, Computer Freelance.

Recruitment Agencies

James Baker Associates,
32 Savile Row, London, W1X 1AG. 071 439 9311

Barnett Consulting Group Ltd.,
Providence House, River Street, Windsor, Berks, SL4 1QT. 0753 856723

Beechwood Recruitment Limited,
221 High Street, London, W3 9BY.

CC & CP International Ltd.,
26-28 Bedford Row, London, WC1R 4HF. 071 242 8998

Consultancy International Ltd.,
40-41 Pall Mall, London, SW1Y 5JG.

MDA Computer Group,
Sceptre House, 169-173 Regent Street, London, W1R 7FB. 071 439 7871

Merton Associates,
Merton House, 70 Grafton Way, London, W1P 5LN.

Swan Recruitment Contracts Division,
Megna House, 48 The Frithe, Wrexham, Slough, SL2 5SU. 0753 577151
This last firm is mainly involved in placements for senior technical/computer/systems programming staff.

Firms with Possibility of Placements Abroad

International Computers Ltd.,
Bridge House, Fulham, London, SW6 3JX.

Logica,
64 Newman Street, London, W1A 4SE.

Cray Research UK Ltd.,
Cray House, London Road, Bracknell, Berks, RG12 2SY.

Construction

We must not fall prey to the popular misconception of

construction offering employment of a primarily manual nature. Not so, and in Canada, as for all advanced countries, construction continues to offer employment of many widely differing varieties including: site managers, site engineers, plant engineers, electricians, quantity surveyors, structural engineers, stores managers, finance professionals, personnel and administration managers, catering staff, and so on.

Most engineering professionals weigh in at a low 1 on the points table, amongst them highway engineers, irrigation and drainage engineers, pipeline engineers, soil and water-resources engineers. Most other professionals in the fields of such as recruitment, financial services and so on, fare no better than their fellow professionals in engineering – still accorded that low '1' to contribute towards their goal.

Journals and Publications

'Construction News', 'Building Today', 'Contract Journal'.

Recruitment Agencies

Anders Glaser Wills,
International Personnel Consultants, 134 High Street, Southampton, SO1 OBR. 0703 223511

Beechwood Recruitment Ltd.,
221 High Street, London, W3 9BY.

Grange Selection,
1 Jubilee Road, Chelsfield, Orpington, Kent, BR6 7QZ.

Consultancy

'Consultancy' covers a very, very wide range of professions indeed, and though Canada is not short of experienced and highly qualified staff in most sectors of industry, commerce and whatever other field one might require the services of specialist consultants, there are still openings for Britons to take up such employment.

Amongst the many specialties for which consultants may be required for whatever duration are included the following: health care, medicine and medical science, engineering, management, planning, agriculture, transport, economics, leisure, tourism and so on.

We can therefore but draw the readers' attention to several firms known to recruit or second consultancy staff to various parts of the world, and provide where possible details relating to professional associations and journals available.

Reference

The British Consultants Bureau,
1 Westminster Palace Gardens, 1-7 Artillery Row, London, SW1P
  1RJ. 071 222 3651
This organisation publishes a list of approximately 500 British
based consultancy firms operating on an international basis.

Professional Associations

Association of Consulting Engineers,
Alliance House, Caxton Street, London, SW1H OQL.

Management Consultancies Association,
11 West Halkin Street, London, SW1 8JZ.

Useful Addresses

Consulting Engineers

Ove Arup Partnership,
13 Fitzroy Street, London, W1P 6BQ.

Sir Alexander Gibb and Partners,
Earley House, London Road, Earley, Reading, RG6 1BL.

Sir M MacDonald & Partners,
Demeter House, Station Road, Cambridge, CB1 2RS.

Sir Owen Williams and Partners,
41 Whitcombe Street, London, WC2 7DT.

Diplomatic Services

A few vacancies do occur in the diplomatic services for those
usually with high academic and professional qualifications, though it
is impossible to be specific on what opportunities might be available
at any point in time.

Those interested in a career in the diplomatic services should
therefore obtain further information and application forms from:

**The Recruitment Section, Personnel Policy Department, Foreign
  and Commonwealth Office,**
3 Central Buildings, Matthew Parker Street, London, SW1H 9NL.
  071 233 5244

Domestic Work

Domestic employees such as gardeners, nannies, housekeepers,
chauffeurs and butlers are in particular demand in Quebec, where
the houseproud nationals are much more than happy to relinquish

everyday mundane housekeeping duties to some other person, particularly if that person comes complete with British accent.

Not of course everyone's top choice for a new career, and not one with the exception of nannies and au pairs, to generally find a large proportion of Britons seeking access. But the fact remains that once granted entry to Canada for whatever reason, whether as dependent or independent migrants, or else for the purposes of retiring there, a great many expatriates make their second or part-time incomes from this particular form of employment. Most such vacancies are advertised in local and provincial Canadian newspapers as well as displayed on notice boards in job centres.

One firm recruiting regularly in London, for positions in Canada, in particular Quebec, is:

Brownstein, Brownstein & Associates
of Montreal. Tel: 514 939 9559

Special Note

See also 'Nannying/Au Pair' for details of firms usually offering placements to domestic workers.

Recruitment Agencies

Allied Agency,
35 Piccadilly, London, W1V 9PB. 071 408 2281

International/Childcare Domestic Directory,
Galentinas Directory, PO Box 51181, GR 145.10, Greece.
This organisation maintains a register of staff interested in worldwide positions as nannies, mothers' helps, butlers and general domestic duties.

The Nightingale Agency,
17 Charnwood Grove, West Bridgford, Nottingham, NG2 7NT.

Engineering

As might be expected from so advanced a country, there is a constant demand for highly qualified engineering professionals in the many varied sectors requiring their services: aerospace, airports, water-resources, highways and heating being but a few of many, many engineering specialties that unfortunately earn just a '1' on the Canadian points table for immigration purposes. Canada is quite capable of providing highly trained staff from within her own educational system.

Engineering in the heavy industrial sense, might bring some opportunities for intending migrants, with machinists, tool and gauge inspectors and gear inspectors all scoring on the points table at that mid-way level of 5 points towards that 70 required for status as independent migrants.

Recruitment Agencies

ARA International,
17-19 Maddox Street, London, W1R OEY.

Benny Electronics Ltd.,
1A Telford Road, Ferndown Industrial Estate, Wimborne, Dorset, BH21 7QN.

Employment Placement and Training Ltd.,
44-48 Hide Hill, Berwick-upon-Tweed, Northumberland, TD15 1AB.

Inter Engineering (Consultancy) Ltd.,
22-24 Buckingham Palace Road, London, SW1W OQP.

Professional Associations

The Institution of Electrical Engineers,
2 Savoy Place, London, WC2R OBL.
This association produces a document for members, entitled 'Working Overseas' in which are contained job vacancies, along with useful information on living and working in various countries.

The Canadian Council of Professional Engineers,
116 Albert Street, Suite 401, Ottawa, Ontario.
In Quebec: 2020 University, 14th Floor, Montreal, Quebec, H3A 2A5.

Fish and Game Commissions, Wildlife and National Parks, etc.

In the many reserves given over to preservation of Canada's fine specimens of wildlife and other natural resources, plentiful job opportunities present themselves, ranging from unskilled labouring jobs to highly skilled professional occupations.

Sadly though, for Britons at least, even the highest qualified scientists who find their specialty featuring significantly in the day-to-day running of these reserves, will discover that Canada can quite adequately cope with filling any vacancies that might result from within its own workforce, consequently giving them a token '1' on the points scale for prospective independent status migrants.

Useful Addresses

Alberta Department of Energy and Natural Resources,
Fish and Wildlife Division, 9915 – 108th Street, Edmonton, T5K
2C9.

British Columbia Ministry of the Environment,
Fish and Wildlife Branch, Parliament Buildings, Victoria, VBV
1X5..

Manitoba Department of Natural Resources,
1495 St. James Street, Winnipeg, R3H OW9.

New Brunswick Department of Natural Resources,
Fish and Wildlife Branch, Centennial Building, PO Box 6000,
Fredericton, E3B 5H1.

Newfoundland Department of Culture,
Recreation and Youth (Wildlife Division), 146-148 Forest Road,
St. John's, A1C 1A8.

Newfoundland Department of Fisheries,
Water Street, St.John's, A1C 5T7.

Nova Scotia Department of Lands and Forests,
(Wildlife Division), Toronto-Dominion Bank Building, 1791
Barrington Street, PO Box 698, Halifax, B3J 2T9.

Nova Scotia Department of Fisheries,
Maritime Centre, Box 2223, Halifax, B3J 3C4.

Ontario Ministry of Natural Resources,
Outdoor Recreation Group, Whitney Block, Parliament Buildings,
Toronto, M7A 1W3.

Prince Edward Island Department of Fisheries,
Shaw Building, PO Box 2000, Charlottetown, C1A 7N8.

Quebec Ministere Du Leosir,
De La Chasse Et De La Peche, 150 est boul, St-Cyrille, Quebec
City, Quebec, G1R 4Y3.

Saskatchewan Tourism and Renewable Resources,
3211 Albert Street, Regina, S4S 5W6.

North West Territories Department of Renewable Resources,
(Fish and Wildlife Service), Yellowknife, N.W.T. X1A 2L9.

Yukon Department of Renewable Resources,
(Wildlife Branch), PO Box 2703, Whitehorse, Yukon Territory,
Y1A 2C6.

Fishing and Hunting

One of Canada's major industries, fishing in particular employs a large proportion of the workforce. Not a career that might facilitate easy access to Canada, though there might well be openings for those deciding to change the course of their employment from within the country.

Hunting where allowed, offers employment to a relatively small number of nationals.

Forestry

Over half of British Columbia and Quebec is forested. Much of the Yukon, and a large proportion of many other provinces is similarly given over to forestation from which Canada owes a great deal of its income from domestic and external sources.

Forestry provides jobs for thousands of citizens, and one might be forgiven for concluding that opportunities exist by the score for those not averse to hard work and long hours. Sadly this is not the case, for the loggers' wages are exceedingly high in comparison to the national average wage. Labour turnover rates are therefore very low indeed, and the queue of Canadian nationals and landed immigrants willing to jump into those few vacancies at virtually a moment's notice, virtually guarantees that few if any foreign labourers or intending immigrants will find work awaiting them here.

Some opportunities do however fall vacant in Canada's replanting projects, a massive and ongoing scheme designed to replace what the logger has taken from the land. Those interested in temporary or permanent work in this area should look under 'Planting Contractors' in Canada's 'Yellow Pages' or else approach forestry offices direct or in writing.

Hotel & Catering

Canada's hotel and catering sector is not only large and expanding; it is also widely diversified, primarily as a result of the country's rich multi-cultural heritage. In outlying areas one might find accommodation and catering facilities of the most basic type; in the Yukon and Northwest territories for instance, such services might come courtesy of the local Indian and Eskimo communities; perhaps just one small hotel, boarding house or Inuit co-operative is available to cater for the needs of visitors to the region. For that visitor the service and hospitality will prove exemplary, but as for job opportunities? Forget it!

A different story entirely is to be told in the major cities located along Canada's border with the United States, where hotels and restaurants though still offering much by way of fast food and basic accommodations facilities, also provide the pleasure seeking tourist and national with a truly sumptuous supply of up-market restaurants of almost every ethnic variety one might consider, and an equally impressive display of top of the range hotel facilities.

The range of opportunities available in Canada's thriving hotel and catering trade are similarly impressive, ranging from cooks to receptionists, hotel managers to bar tenders, waitresses to chambermaids and so on.

Of particular interest to the intending immigrant, is the fact that chefs and qualified cooks currently feature at a high of 10 points on the immigration points scale. Those jobs currently accorded a 10 include the following:

> General chef-cook
> Head chef
> Banquet chef
> Small establishment cook
> Patissier chef
> Saucier chef
> Rotisseur chef
> Domestic cook
> Garde-manger chef
> Entremetier chef
> Caterer
> Instruction cook
> Kosher foods cook
> Working sous chef
> Foreign foods cook
> First cook
> Therapeutic diet cook
> Camp cook

As is the case for many other parts of the world, wages in the hotel and catering industry can prove extremely low; hence bartenders, waiters and waitresses all depend heavily upon tips from satisfied customers.

Details of jobs requiring higher or professional qualifications are advertised in Canadian newspapers and in trade and professional publications. The intending employee can also take the opportunity to place 'situations wanted' advertisements in these same publications, or else might peruse Canadian job centres for details of current vacancies.

The intending employee can instead take the option of approaching major hotels and food chains direct. Given that labour turnover can be high amongst the lower paid jobs in this industry, there is usually a very good chance of finding one's speculative letter has in fact been placed on file ready to contact potentially suitable employees at peak times, or during periods of heavy staff shortages.

Most tourist offices are able to provide details of hotels, restaurants and other such establishments, located in various parts of Canada.

Reference

'**ABC Worldwide Hotel Guide**' lists leading hotels throughout the world, to which the intending working holidaymaker or hopeful migrant may make direct application. This useful book is published by:

ABC International,
World Timetable Centre, Church Street, Dunstable, Beds, LU5 4HB.

'**Agents' Hotel Gazetteer**', published by CHG Publications, lists a wide range of hotels in specific locations, and is available for consultation in most main reference libraries.

Journals and Publications

'Caterer and Hotelkeeper'

Recruitment Agencies

VIP International,
17 Charing Cross Road, London, WC2H OEP. 071 930 0541
This organisation recruits qualified staff, usually with four years' minimum experience, to worldwide positions in the catering and hospitality trade.

Legal Profession

As for her neighbour the United States, Canada is home to a growing band of highly qualified, highly experienced, and highly specialised lawyers to provide for the many facets of her varied business, social and cultural infrastructure.

Again due to its advanced educational system, bolstered by the requirements to train individuals specifically with the country's own legal codes in mind, Canada provides well for the legal profession from within the population.

The country does however seem to be in short supply of legal secretaries and court reporters, for whom a point of 5 is accorded to those seeking entry as independent migrants.

Qualified lawyers up to the age of thirty years might however find their services in some demand, often on a short term basis. Such secondments to various positions in most parts of the world are often effected by:

Offshore Specialist Appointments,
Tower Hill Steps, 16 Le Brodage, St. Peter Port, Guernsey.

Recruitment Agencies

Meredith Scott Associates,
Legal Selection Consultant, 17 Fleet Street, London, EC4 1AA.

Law Personnel,
95 Aldwych, London, WC2B 4JF. 071 242 1281

Reuter Simkin Ltd.,
26 – 29 Bedford Row, London, WC1R 4HL.

Manufacturing

A rapidly expanding manufacturing and industrial sector offers many opportunities to nationals as well as intending foreign workers. Motor vehicles, telecommunications, textiles, iron and steel, industrial and agricultural machinery, food processing, and electronics are but a few of the many specialties of the Canadian manufacturing industry.

Again, one often finds Canada well able to cater for her staffing requirements from indigenous sources. This sector does however present many job opportunities for landed immigrants and their dependants, if not in assisting their passage to their new country, then at least providing for career changes in future years.

Recruitment Agencies

Grange Selection,
1 Jubilee Road, Chelsfield, Orpington, Kent, BR6 7QZ.

Wrightson Wood Ltd.,
11 Grosvenor Place, London, SW1X 7HA.
This latter firm specialises in worldwide placements for senior managers in the manufacturing industry.

Medical, Nursing, Health Care and Social Sector Professions

Canada's health care and social sectors are extremely well advanced, and one might easily be led to believe that the country would experience few problems in catering for its own staffing requirements in these areas. This however is not apparently the case, and one finds the immigration points table burdened with a long, long list of health care professionals for whose services and skills that high score of '10' is accorded.

Amongst those professionals currently scoring so highly are:

Audiologist
Speech pathologist
Clinical occupational therapy specialist
Occupational therapist
Physiotherapist
Remedial gymnast
Respiratory technologist

Others weighing in a little lower on the points table, with a score awarded of 5 points, are:

Social work supervisor
Parole officer
Probation officer
Social worker
Addiction counsellor
Half-way house supervisor
Child care worker
Geriatric-activities aide

Useful Addresses and Sources of Further Information

Canadian Dietetic Association,
480 University Avenue, Suite 604, Toronto, M5G 1VZ.
Publishes a list of regulations and educational requirements for dietitians considering employment in Canada.

The Canadian Medical Association,
Box 8650, Ottawa, Ontario, K1G OG8.
This professional body publishes 'The Canadian Medical Association Journal', wherein is contained a large classified opportunities section. A free leaflet 'Medical Practice in Canada' provides information of interest to those intending to work in Canada, and lists also the addresses of provincial Medical Associations and appropriate qualifications and registration requirements.

Pharmacists are obliged to register with provincial authorities. Candidates should contact:

The Pharmacy Examining Board of Canada,
Suite 603, 123 Edward Street, Toronto, Ontario, Canada, M5G 1E2.

In Quebec:

Pharmaciens du Quebec,
266 Notre Dame Ouest, Montreal, Quebec, H2Y IT5.

Nurses seeking employment in Canada, should contact the following groups where advice is available concerning qualifications, experience and jobs available in most countries:

Universal Care,
Chester House, 9 Windsor End, Beaconsfield, Bucks, HP9 2JJ.

Recruitment Agencies

International Hospitals Group (IBG),
Stoke Park, Stock Poges, Slough, Berkshire, SL2 4HS.
(Specialise in most medical and health care professional placements)

Mediservice,
Bournemouth International Airport, Christchurch, Dorset, BH23
  6EB. 0202 572271
Specialists in placement of nurses on a worldwide basis

Medic International,
4 Thameside Centre, Kew Bridge Road, Brentford, Middlesex,
  TW8 OHB. 081 568 4300
Specialises in the placement of doctors to worldwide positions

Dorothy J Hopkins,
Claridge House, 29 Barnes High Street, London, SW13 9LW. 081
  876 8666
Specialises in the placement of doctors, nurses and health care adminstrators to positions worldwide

Flexcareer Ltd.,
59 The Vale, London, W3 7RR. 071 749 3013
Specialises in placements for nursing personnel

Professional Associations

The Society of Chiropodists,
53 Wellbeck Street, London, W1M 7HE.

The International Dental Federation,
64 Wimpole Street, London, W1M 8AL.
The IDF publishes 'The Handbook of Regulations of Dental
Practice', detailing addresses and sources of further information of use to those contemplating working overseas

The British Medical Association,
Tavistock Square, London, WC1H 9JP.

The Royal College of Nursing,
Cavendish Square, London, W1M OAB.

Mining

Canada's rich reserves of minerals lie largely untapped, guaranteeing work virtually indefinitely in the field of mining, be it coal, nickel, zinc, copper, gold, or any of the many other deposits existing in plentiful supply in most provinces.

The mining sector offers wide ranging job and career opportunities, from manual to administrative, and on to the higher echelons of metallurgy, geophysics, and a host of other highly skilled and just as highly paid professional disciplines.

Reference

'**The Mining International Yearbook',** available in public reference libraries.

'**International Mining: A Career for Professional Engineers',** is available in all main reference libraries.

'**Financial Times Mining International Year Book',** is edited by J Banfield, and published by Longman.

Journals and Publications

'Mining Journal'.

Recruitment Agencies

Hunter Personnel,
PO Box 564, Verwood, Wimborne, Dorset, BH21 6YB.

British Mining Consultants,
Mill Lane, Huthwaite, Sutton in Ashfield, Notts., NG17 2NS.

Anders Glaser Wills,
International Recruitment Consultants, 4 Maddison Court,
  Maddison Street, Southampton, SO1 OBU.

C C & P International Ltd.,
26-28 Bedford Row, London, WC1R 4HF. 071 242 8998

Grange Selection,
1 Jubilee Road, Chelsfield, Orpington, Kent, BR6 7QZ.

Professional and Mining Associations

The Mining Association of the United Kingdom,
6 St. James Square, London, SW1Y 4LD.
Formerly 'The Overseas Mining Association', this particular body

is able to provide a complete list of individual worldwide companies to which the interested job applicant might direct his attention.

British Columbia and Yukon Chamber of Mines,
840 West Hastings Street, Vancouver, BC, Canada, V6C 1C8. This association publishes a list of mining firms in British Columbia, the Yukon and Northwest Territories.

Mineral Industry Manpower and Careers Unit,
Prince Consort Road, London, SW7 2BP. 071 584 7397

Nannying/Au Pair

The Canadian au pair system so well-established, no doubt speaks volumes for the heavy French influence prevailing in many parts of the country.

So popular are British nannies and au pairs, that many nationals and government officials believe their Canadian counterparts are being unfairly deprived of jobs. Consequently immigration laws in respect of nannies and au pairs from other parts of the world were tightened and various restrictions placed on the movement of such employees into Canada, including a requirement that all taking such employment must remain in the country for at least one year.

Several agencies are available to arrange placements to young women willing to offer their services as mother's helps and child minders in exchange for living accommodation and board, and usually with a predetermined level of pocket money being provided. Amongst such agencies are:

Aaron Employment Agency,
Suite C, The Courtyard, Stanley Road, Off Camden Road, Tunbridge Wells, Kent, TN1 2RJ. 0892 546601

Anglia Au Pair Agency,
70 Southsea Avenue, Leigh-on-Sea, Essex, SS9 2BJ. 0702 471648

Anglo Pair Agency,
40 Wavertree Road, Streatham Hill, London, SW2 3SP. 081 674 3605

Avalon Agency,
30 Queen's Road, Brighton, East Sussex, BN1 3XA. 0273 26866

Baxter's Agency,
PO Box 12, Peterborough, Cambs, PE3 6JN.

Bees Knees,
296 Sandycombe Road, Kew Gardens, Richmond, Surrey, TW9
3NG. 081 876 7039

Euro Employment Centre,
42 Upper Union Arcade, Bury, Lancashire, BL9 OQF. 061 797
6400

European Nannies,
5 Wimblehurst Road, Horsham, West Sussex, RH12 2EA. 0403
52372

The Experiment for International Living,
'Otesaga', Upper Wyche, Malvern, Worcs, WR14 4EN. 0684
562577

Janet White Employment Agency,
67 Jackson Avenue, Leeds, LS8 1NS. 0532 666507

Just the Job,
8 Musters Road, West Bridgford, Nottingham, NG2 6JA. 0602
813224

Nash Personnel Services,
Homelands House, Bines Road, Partridge Green, Horsham,
Sussex, RH13 8EQ. 0403 711436

Norfolk Care Search Agency,
19 London Road, Downham Market, Norfolk, PE38 9BJ. 0366
384448

North South Agency,
28 Wellington Road, Hastings, East Sussex, TN34 3RN. 0424 422
364

Pre-Select Staff Agency,
924 Stratford Road, Birmingham, B11 4BT.

Universal Care,
1 Chester House, 9 Windsor End, Beaconsfield, Bucks, HP9 2JJ.
0494 678811

Special Note

In many parts, particularly Quebec, the demand for British
nannies is high. One recruitment firm whose representatives visit
London on a monthly basis to interview prospective staff is:

Brownstein, Brownstein & Associates,
based in Montreal. Tel: 514 939 9559

Oil and Gas

Oil and gas companies are amongst the few sectors to offer ongoing opportunities for employees working through the entire gamut from exploration to finished production. Jobs are many and varied, many of them specialist positions such as might already have been mentioned in other categories within this section; engineers, consultants, accountants, and so on.

Amongst the many other specialties for which openings regularly occur are such as pilots, geologists, administrators, clerical and secretarial staff, researchers, and so on.

This is another field in which those opportunities, so many and varied, leave no alternative but to point the reader in the general direction of the major recruitment agencies and sources of job vacancies, reference books, and employing companies.

Reference

'Oil and Gas International Yearbook', giving details of the world's oil and gas companies, is available in most major reference libraries.

Major Companies

The readers' attention is directed towards those companies listed at the end of this section, some based in Britain, others in Canada, some in various other parts of the world, but all with subsidiaries or separate commercial operations in Canada. In particular the following companies are of interest to those contemplating entering Canada's oil and gas industry:

Petro-Canada,
PO Box 2844, Calgary, Alberta, Canada, T2P 3E3.
Petro-Canada Resources is that section which deals with exploration and processing of crude oil, natural gas and natural gas liquids, Petro-Canada Products refines, distributes and markets petroleum products.

Pan-Canadian Petroleum Ltd.,
Pan Canadian Plaza, PO Box 2850, Calgary, Alberta, Canada, T2P 2S5.

British Petroleum Co Plc.,
Britannic House, Moor Lane, London, EC2 9BU.

Conoco (UK) Ltd.,
Park House, 116 Park Street, London, W1Y 4NN.

Kuwait Oil Co.,
54 St James's Street, London, W1Y 4NN.

Mobil,
54-60 Victoria Street, London, SW1E 6QB.

Phillips Petroleum,
Phillips Quadrant, 35 Guildford Road, Woking, Surrey, GU22
7QT.

Shell International,
Shell Centre, London, SE1 7NA.

Texaco,
1 Knightsbridge Green, London, SW1X 7JQ.

Total Oil Marine Plc.,
Berkeley Square House, Berkeley Square, London, W1X 6LT.

Teaching/University/Education/Academic

The Canadian Teacher's Federation,
110 Argyle Avenue, Ottawa, Ontario, K2P 1B4.
Issues a free booklet 'Teaching in Canada', providing much useful
information for intending expatriates.

Other organisations of interest to teachers intending to work in
Canada include the following:

The Canadian Education Association,
252 Bloor Street W, 8th Floor, Toronto, Ontario, M5S 1V5.
Issues leaflet 'Information for Teachers thinking of coming to
Canada'.

Computerised Teacher Registry, British Columbia School Trustees'
Association,
1155 West 8th Avenue, Vancouver, British Columbia, V6H 1C5.

Department of Education,
PO Box 6000, Fredericton, New Brunswick, E3B 5HI.

Teachers hoping to find employment in particular parts of Canada
might contact:

Administration and Professional Certification,
Professional Certification Section, 227-1200 Portage Avenue,
Winnipeg, Manitoba, R3G OT5.

Department of Education,
PO Box 6000, Fredericton, New Brunswick, E3B 5HI.

The Director of Personnel,
Government of the Northwest Territories, Yellowknife, NWT
X1A 2L9.

For those interested in teaching in the private sector information is available from:

The Executive Secretary, Canadian Association of Independent Schools,
c/o Stanstead College, Stanstead, Quebec, JOB 3EO.

University teaching personnel might refer to the following sources for opportunities available:

CAUT Bulletin, Canadian Association of University Teachers,
c/o 75 Albert Street, Suite 1001, Ottawa, Ontario, Canada, K1P 5E7.

University Affairs, Association of Universities and Colleges of Canada,
Publications Office, 151 Slater Street, Ottawa, Canada, K1P 5N1. (The AUCC is also able to offer a list of addresses of Canadian universities and colleges of higher education)

Universities' vacancies are advertised in 'University Affairs', available ten times a year from:

The Association of Universities and Colleges of Canada,
Publications Office, 151 Slater Street, Ottawa, Canada, K1P 5NI.

Tourism and Travel

Not surprisingly, tourism features heavily in the Canadian way of life, despite the fact that the majority of tourists come from not too distant a location; in 1987 of almost 39 million visitors to Canada, it was estimated that 37 million were United States citizens or visitors for whom that lower part of the continent featured as first destination on their itineraries.

Tourism presents many openings for nationals and working holidaymakers amongst them: couriers, canoeing instructors, swimming instructors, and instructors for many other sports. Amongst suitable agencies for such placements are:

Camp White Pine,
40 Lawrence Avenue West, Toronto, Ontario, Canada, M5M 1A4.

Acorn Venture Ltd.,
137 Worcester Road, Hagley, Stourbridge, DY9 ONW.

Exodus Expeditions,
9 Weir Road, London, SW12 OLT. 081 675 7996

Mark Warner,
20 Kensington Church Street, London, W8 4EP.

VIP International,
17 Charing Cross Road, London, WC2H OEP. 071 930 0541
Mainly involved in placements for hotel and catering professionals
with at least 4 years' experience.

Casual/Holiday Work

(See also 'Tourism', 'Agriculture', 'Hotel and Catering', etc.)

Workcamp and volunteer opportunities are available throughout
the country, again with a great number of agencies available to
provide suitable placements. Amongst them one finds the following:

Frontiers Foundation/Operation Beaver,
2615 Danforth Avenue, Suite 203, Toronto, Ontario, Canada,
M4C 1LS.

International Voluntary Service,
162 Upper New Walk, Leicester, LE1 7QA. 0532 406787

Christian Movement for Peace,
Bethnal Green United Reformed Church, Pott Street, London,
E2 OEF. 071 729 1877

International Voluntary Service,
162 Upper New Walk, Leicester, LE1 7QA. 0533 549430

United Nations Association International Youth Service,
Temple of Peace, Cathays Park, Cardiff, CF1 3AP. 0222 223088

Opportunities in children's camps and on playscheme projects
may be arranged via:

British Universitities North America Club (BUNAC),
16 Bowling Green Lane, London, EC1R OBD. 071 251 3472

GAP Activity Projects Ltd.,
Gap House, 44 Queens Road, Reading, Berkshire, RG1 4BB.
0734 594914

Miscellaneous Recruitment Agencies

Recruitment International,
2nd floor, Copthall Tower House, Station Parade, Harrogate,
HG1 1IS.
This particular firm specialises in many professions and job
openings on a worldwide basis.

Finally

As has been said on so many occasions, this is the world's largest
country, and a highly advanced one at that. Consequently it proves

virtually impossible to generalise on the main opportunities available for employment in Canada. We can, as we hope we have accomplished, bring but a few of the main sectors of employment to the readers' attention.

Directory – Main Industries in Canada

If one word were to be selected to sum up the overall structure of Canadian industry, one that would also explain the reason for the country's enviable economic stability, that word must surely be 'diversified'. Canada is a land of many varied industrial and commercial activities, perhaps more varied than any other country of the world.

From its traditional role in agriculture, fishing, fur trading and mining of minerals and other resources in which the country is particularly well-endowed, Canada extended her activities into textile production, food processing, manufacturing of vehicles and vehicle parts, and finally included in her wide ranging portfolio of industrial activities the more modern sectors of aerospace, computer technology, electronics and telecommunications.

But it wasn't until as late as the 1950s that Canada actually came to exploit other than her traditional agricultural, fishing and fur trading industries. In the 20 years from 1950, Canada experienced a growth and prosperity such as it had never before experienced.

Industrialisation in the modern sense took Canada by storm, high technology industries came into being as management and production methods became ever more sophisticated and in tune with the needs of both domestic and international markets. At around the same time, Canada's already magnificent natural mineral resources were supplemented by the discovery of massive deposits of iron in Labrador and vast reserves of oil in most parts of the country.

Structure of industry bears close resemblance to that of the United Kingdom and other established industrial centres of world activity. There are many successful Canadian firms operating solely on a regional basis, others offering products and services limited to the domestic market, and yet a further group of international companies whose operations spread to numerous other countries. Many such Canadian firms have a hundred or more bases in the United Kingdom alone.

In Canada there are examples of virtually every industry one finds in the United Kingdom, though obviously many of them operate on a grander scale, even those that cater primarily or exclusively for domestic markets.

In this section we can but present a selection of the main types of industry to which Canada owes its healthy economic climate. Research in any public reference library will expand upon this list for that reader interested in the industrial sector for the purpose of seeking employment, establishing business links, or for whatever other reason.

Agriculture

Since much of Canada lies to the extreme north, only 7% or so of land is suitable for farming; three-quarters of that small amount lying in the western Canadian prairies, colloquially referred to as 'the world's bread basket', a name well deserved for the mass of grain and cereal produced in the region.

Amongst the country's most important cereal crops are included: barley, oats and rye. Canada is one of the world's primary exporters of cereal, much of it from her prairie regions. An abundant land surface also yields plentiful supplies of fruits, beef and potatoes, the latter to which tiny Prince Edward Island owes its worldwide fame.

Most working farms are concentrated in a few relatively small regions principally around Ontario, Southern Quebec and New Brunswick. Grain production, dairying, fruit farming, fur production and ranching, all flourish in that small amount of arable land available in Canada.

Saskatchewan is one of the country's primary wheat growing regions, and also produces much of Canada's livestock for domestic consumption and exportation.

In Quebec, cereal and dairy products are the main agricultural products. Remaining loyal to the methods and traditions of their ancestors, in the Yukon, Northwest Territories and Saskatchewan, the fur trade remains a viable and significant part of respective economies.

In Ontario, the near tropical climate is responsible for extensive tobacco and fruit production, the former of which is of the highest quality, usually the Virginia variety to which the country owes a significant proportion of its income from outside sources, including the United Kingdom.

Fishing and Fisheries

Bordering on three oceans, fishing assumes great importance to the Canadian economy. The country boasts a truly massive fish catch; in 1986, figures released showed a 1.66 million ton yield, and profits in the region of $271 million owed to its salmon catch; $218 million for cod; $243 million from lobster, and a comparatively low $74 million from the humble herring.

Canada is the world's leading exporter of fish and seafood, much of it owed to the long and winding coastlines of the Eastern Atlantic provinces, where mainland shores and dense archipelago regions make for an economy for which fishing is the major benefactor, accounting for the majority of employment in the region.

Fishing is also vitally important to the economies of New Brunswick and Nova Scotia, and from the extensive fishing grounds of the 'Grand Banks' of Newfoundland comes a major proportion of Canada's annual fish catch, in this case revealing itself primarily in bountiful supplies of salmon, char and pike.

Forestry

(See also 'Paper and Pulp Production')

One of the first things that springs to most people's minds about Canada is the image of the lumberjack and his partner the logger. This in fact is not surprising, since 35% of Canada's massive surface is covered in dense green forests. Much of that land to the extreme north and not suitable for farming, is forested mainly with coniferous specimens and largely inaccessible during the coldest months. River systems however, go some way towards alleviating the situation, when activity is greatly increased during the 'warmer' months and timber hastily transported to more hospitable areas for processing.

Heavy exploitation of this, one of Canada's most significant assets, is leading to an identity crisis with which many citizens can not come to terms. On the one hand, they realise their country's relatively stable economy owes much to those end products of tree-felling and heavy logging industries; on the other they understand only too well that the real scenic beauty of trees, many of them hundreds of years old, once reduced to a wasteland of rubble presents far too high a price to pay.

Amongst the main secondary industries are lumber, pulp and paper production, paper-processing, newsprint, plywood, logs, and timber supplies for use in the building sector.

Much of the logging industry centres in the Yukon, whilst heavy timber processing features highly in the economy of British Columbia where around one-quarter of all North America's timber supplies originate.

Some 85% of New Brunswick is densely forested, providing for a thriving paper and paper-processing industry that ironically impedes access to vast reserves of lead, copper and zinc below ground.

The forests of Newfoundland also yield enormous supplies of timber, again making for a thriving domestic paper and paper-processing industry to which a great many inhabitants owe their livelihood. One might be forgiven for believing that here one will find plentiful job opportunities in scenic and peaceful surroundings, but this would be an entirely inaccurate assumption, for loggers' and timber operatives' wages are incredibly high and job vacancies consequently very, very thin on the ground.

If those recently mentioned forestation levels seem high, consider then the province of Ontario, home to heavily populated cities Ottawa and Toronto. It might then come as some surprise to discover that over 90% of the province is covered in forests, and that not only is forestry, timber and logging of vital importance to the economy of the province, but that Ontario is also the most heavily industrialised of provinces.

In Quebec over half of land-surface is given over to trees, again providing ample job opportunities for locals in timber, logging and ultimately the paper, pulp and paper processing industries.

That image then of the brightly-coated lumberjack might indeed be the closest one is ever likely to come to a description of the average Canadian, given that so much of the workforce is employed in the many industries revolving around timber.

For reasons far too obvious to mention, timber is one of Canada's major exports, and mainstay of the economy on a domestic and external basis.

Iron & Steel

Though iron and steel had long contributed significantly to the nation's economy, it wasn't until the 1950s that untapped reserves of iron in Labrador were exploited. Though the existence of iron in this particular area had long been established, very little investigation had taken place as to the extent of whatever reserves were available. When that task was accomplished in the 1950s the true measure of Labrador's valuable reserves became known, leading to rapid plans for exploitation, the end result contributing dramatically to Canada's economic well-being and industrial expansion from the 1950s onwards.

The 1950s were also to have a tremendous impact on the steel industry, when crude steel production almost doubled between 1959 and 1969, aided more than a little by the opening of the St. Lawrence Seaway in 1959, and the abundant supplies of Labrador's newly-exploited treasure trove of iron ore.

Today, steel production predominates in Montreal. Hamilton and Sault Ste Marie are also amongst the main iron and steel centres.

Iron and steel manufacturing companies flourish in many parts of the country, amongst them a great many British companies, the addresses for which are detailed at the end of this chapter, included amongst them British Steel.

Manufacturing

'Manufacturing' of course, covers a very wide range of activities, from those servicing and resulting from the country's traditional role as agricultural nation to which thousands of food processing and agricultural machinery firms owe their existence, to the more futuristic sectors of computers and electronics.

Agriculture and subsequent food processing accounts for 15% of all manufacturing activity. Montreal is particularly rich in food processing industries, as are the provinces of Manitoba, Alberta and Nova Scotia.

Toronto and Montreal are the chief manufacturing cities. Toronto's specialties are motor vehicles, electrical equipment, chemicals, textiles and aircraft. The country's thriving electronics and electrical industries operate primarily from Toronto. Textiles industries flourish in all well-populated areas, primary amongst them Manitoba, Quebec and Nova Scotia. The latter is also justifiably proud of the contribution its leather processing and leather goods industries make to its own and the country's economy.

In Montreal manufacture centres mainly in the areas of steel, chemicals, textiles, foodstuffs, and petroleum products. Textiles industries operate mainly in and around the cities of Toronto and Montreal; overall the industry along with its resulting stream of clothing manufacturers, accounts for 7% of all income from manufacturing.

Motor vehicle production features prominently in Canada's manufacturing sector, much of it centred in Toronto. In manufacturing terms, it is to the automobile industry that Canada owes much of her increased affluence in the past few decades. Canadian exports of automobiles and automotive products rose significantly during the mid 1960s, much of those products destined for the neighbouring United States. Though developing a healthy climate in the monetary sense, the price many Canadians find too high, in terms of an increased dependence upon their neighbours lower in the North American continent.

Aircraft and aerospace industries are to be found in most heavily industrialised sectors, more conspicuously in and around the city of Toronto.

Amongst major British and international aircraft and aircraft parts companies operating also from bases in Canada are: Airship Industries Ltd., British Aerospace Plc. and Hawker Siddeley Group Plc, addresses for which are detailed later in this chapter.

Industrial and agricultural machinery is important not only for domestic consumption, but features also in income derived from outside sources. Ontario and Alberta produce a large proportion of such equipment and machinery for internal and external consumption, and many similar industries are located in Nova Scotia, and to a lesser extent agricultural and agricultural machinery industries flourish in almost all well populated centres.

The motor vehicle and vehicle parts industry predominates in Toronto, where output accounts for 25% of all manufacturing activities. In 1991 this particular sector of industry brought in $bn 28.9 income from exports.

Industrial supplies feature heavily in Canada's income from outside sources.

Rubber processing and subsequent production of rubber goods are amongst Canada's prime manufacturing sectors.

Ontario in general, and Toronto and Montreal in particular, are amongst the major centres of chemical industrial activities. Amongst major international companies to have bases in Canada are Imperial Chemical Industries Plc. and Brent Chemicals, the addresses for which are provided at the end of this chapter.

More akin to the needs of tomorrow's people, Canada is also amongst one of the world's main producers of computers, computer equipment and software. Also of great significance are the country's many electronics and electrical goods manufacturers, in the latter of which the province of Quebec is particularly active. Amongst major British and international firms operating also within Canada are included: General Electric Company and Thorn EMI Plc.

Amongst those British and international companies from various other specialities, operating from bases within Canada and to whom the reader might direct his or her attention are: Fisons Plc, Grand Metropolitan Plc., Lucas Industries Plc., E D & F Mann Ltd. (Sugar producers), Racal Electronics Plc., Unigate Plc., United Biscuits Plc., Allied-Lyons Plc., and Cadbury Schweppes Plc.

Mining & Quarrying

Canada's proud claim of offering one of the world's highest standards of living to her citizens is owed mainly to her vast mineral reserves, much of which as yet remains untapped. Mining is concentrated on zinc, nickel, gold, silver, iron ore, uranium, copper, cobalt and lead.

Canada's rapid industrial and economic growth from the 1950s onwards, was largely due to the discovery of new mineral reserves, not only the realisation of iron ore deposits in Labrador, but also radium and oil in many other parts of the country.

Canada's primary mining regions are centred in the provinces of Alberta, British Columbia, Saskatchewan and Quebec. Saskatchewan boasts massive reserves of gold, silver and cadmium; Quebec is wealthy in gold, iron and copper reserves; New Brunswick is home to plentiful supplies of lead, copper and zinc, albeit in this particular province mining is severely hindered by the fact that around 85% of the province is covered in heavy forestation. Problems of access to valuable reserves present greater difficulties in those locations within the Arctic Circle, where permanently frost-bound conditions continue to impede access despite ongoing attempts to alleviate such problems.

Canada is of course one of the world's largest producers and exporters of minerals and metals, a position the country quite naturally seeks to retain by means of large injections of capital, employment training programmes, and recruitment specifically designed to improve the skills of those to whom the task of exploitation will be assigned. So well did Canada work towards these objectives, that between 1961 and 1970 the volume of production in the mining sector rose by 75%, an increase that has continued ever since.

All provinces yield abundant supplies of several minerals; hence one finds mining activities existing on a varying scale throughout the whole of Canada, the size of such activities depending obviously upon the extent of reserves available for commercial exploitation, as well as the ease or otherwise of gaining access to sufficient supplies to make for viable mining operations. The Yukon for instance offers abundant supplies of gold, silver, zinc and lead, as well as a climate cold enough to make transportation of whatever one might extract from the land a more than difficult proposition.

Paper and Pulp Production

(See also 'Forestry')

Forestry and timber processing featured as the earliest of the country's commercial activities. In time those industries came to realise the contribution they could make to the developing sectors of publishing, printing and paper processing. Wood pulp and paper industries consequently flourish throughout Canada.

Pulp is turned into newsprint and it is estimated that half of all newspapers in Europe and North America are printed on Canadian paper, much of it originating from the northern coniferous forest belt that stretches the breadth of the country.

Amongst the primary wood pulp and paper processing provinces are Newfoundland, New Brunswick, Ontario, Nova Scotia, Quebec and Saskatchewan.

Doubtless this flourishing sector well explains the preponderance of many Canadian publishing and major newspaper concerns operating throughout the country, and no doubt lies behind the decision of many foreign companies to transfer part or all of their own publishing and printing concerns to Canada.

Petro-Chemicals and Gas

One of the world's primary petroleum-producing countries, Canada's main deposits are to be found in the Interior Plains in the tar sands along Alberta's Athabasca River. From here an extensive network of pipelines carries oil to refineries in southern Canada and the United States.

Though Canada's wealth of petroleum and gas reserves had long been realised, it wasn't until 1947 that the country established itself as an exporter of oil. Gas had contributed to the economy of southern Alberta from the early 1900s, but only from the end of World War II did prospecting of oil and gas achieve a foothold in other provinces. Oil prospecting commenced on a grand and constantly growing scale across the prairie provinces, spurred on by major strikes in Saskatchewan and Manitoba, and more so by the discovery of valuable reserves leading northwards from Alberta to the Mackenzie valley. By the 1960s prospecting was planned for the Arctic Islands, the reward for which came in the early 1970s with the discovery of abundant gas and oil reserves.

The world's longest oil and gas pipelines, over 2,000 miles in length, move crude oil from oilfields and gasfields in all parts to most major cities, and major pipelines several hundred miles in length cross the rugged Rocky Mountains to supply the lowel mainland of British Columbia and the Pacific regions northwest of the United States.

In Montreal, the petroleum industry is one of the mainstays of the city's economy. Much the same can be said of the contribution petroleum makes to the economies of the Northwest Territories, Ontario and Saskatchewan.

Amongst the main producers of natural gas are Alberta, the Northwest Territories and Saskatchewan.

Many British and international oil producers and refiners operate from bases in Canada, addresses for many of which are included at the end of this chapter.

Amongst those firms are included: Conoco (UK) Ltd., Mobil, Phillips Petroleum, Shell International, Texaco, British Gas Plc., The British Petroleum Co. Plc., The Burmah Oil Company, Century Oils, and Costain Group Plc.

Transportation and Transportation Equipment

The largest nation of the world, and one in which the climate and rugged topography renders many regions virtually inaccessible for much of the year, Canada's population depends for its personal and economic well-being on a well-established and efficient system of transportation, as indeed do her commercial, business and industrial sectors.

The vital importance of Canada's transportation system provides employment for a large proportion of the workforce. Automobile and auto parts manufacture we have already considered as crucial to the country's income from exports, as well as the contribution this sector of manufacturing makes towards its country's domestic requirements.

Canada's logging industries, along with pulp, paper processing and mining sectors are heavily reliant upon a well-established and adequately maintained system of roads to service the transportation of their products from primarily outlying parts of the country. Many of these roads are closed to public transportation and reserved exclusively for use by those companies dependent for their existence upon the efficient movement of timber, minerals and secondary products. For transportation of other products between major centres Canada's road system proves highly efficient. Trucking as an industry has in fact increased dramatically since the end of World War II.

To facilitate speed of access between major centres for both public and industrial use, Canada's railway network is one of the most efficient in the world, and again contributes significantly to the jobs market.

Waterways transport a large proportion of goods for both domestic and international trade. Inland shipping routes and canals operate throughout the country, many of them accommodating even the largest of sea going vessels. Numerous ports facilitate transfer of goods carried through inland waterways, before resuming their passage to further domestic or international destinations.

But it is to airways that the overcoming of obstacles presented by Canada's rough terrain and harsh weather conditions is largely credited. Vast distances, roads often snow-blocked for long periods at a time, dangerous winter driving conditions, have led to a system of air transportation for which Canada must surely be the envy of many other countries.

Various airlines operate on domestic and international routes for the transportation of either passengers or cargo, or else a combination of both. Many smaller private airlines operate similar services to industry and public, albeit on a markedly reduced scale, but nevertheless providing a service that not only contributes significantly to their country's economic well-being, but also provides much by way of job opportunities in all parts of the country.

Of course, transportation itself proving so important a feature in the country's economy, industry was quick to seize upon every opportunity to provide for the needs of transportation companies, and consequently production of vehicles and spare parts features prominently in the country's manufacturing sector. Shipbuilding firms operate from most of the milder parts of Canada's extensive coastline, with many British and international firms being represented in their midst. Trains or 'rolling stock' offer industrial and employment opportunities in many parts of the country, predominantly in the province of Quebec.

Finally

We have of course just touched the surface of those industries to which Canada owes her stable and healthy economic climate. Many more industries operate throughout the country, many of them major international companies, some operating in all industrialised areas, other operating instead on a regional basis. The readers' attention is therefore directed towards the many reference books available in major public reference libraries, in which full details will be found of less prominent industries, along with names and addresses of major Canadian, British, foreign and international businesses operating in respective industrial sectors.

Company Directory – Useful Addresses

A. Major Canadian Companies – Addresses in the UK
B. Major UK Companies with Bases or Subsidiaries in Canada

A. Major Canadian Companies – Addresses in the UK

The reader's attention is drawn to the fact that many Canadian companies operate also from bases within the United Kingdom. Many such firms are listed in those trade directories and sources of additional information to which reference is made in 'Live and Work in Canada'.

We can do little other than present a small selection of representative firms to which the reader might make application for employment. In selecting those firms for inclusion in this section, attention has focussed on larger organisations, primarily those with several operations in Britain. For full details of addresses in the United Kingdom the reader is advised to contact the company's head office in Canada.

* Details in brackets indicate the company's British trading name.

Alberta Energy Co. Ltd,
2400- 639 5th Avenue South West, Calgary, Alberta, T2P DM9.
(Chieftain Exploration (UK) Ltd.)

Alcan Aluminium Ltd,
1188 Sherbrooke Street West, Montreal, Quebec, H3A 3G2.
(Alcan – various names, British Alcan Aluminium Plc – approaching 100 divisions in the United Kingdom)

B P Canadian Holdings Ltd,
Suite 2100, 855 – 2nd Street West, Calgary, Alberta, T2P 4J9.
(Supertest Petroleum (UK) Ltd)

Canada Life Assurance Co,
330 University Avenue, Toronto, Ontario, M5G 1R8.
(Various operations in the United Kingdom usually with name commencing 'Canada Life')

Confederation Life Insurance Co,
321 Bloor Street East, Toronto, Ontario, M4W 1H1.
(Various operations in the United Kingdom)

Crown Inc,
120 Bloor Street East, Toronto, Ontario, M4W 1B8.
(Various operations in the United Kingdom usually incorporating the name 'Crown')

Fednav Ltd,
Suite 2600, 600 de la Gauchetiere West, Montreal, Quebec, H3B 4M3.
(Six shipping operations in the United Kingdom, under the heading 'Fednav')

Henlys Group Plc,
3400 Stock Exchange Towers, PO Box 455, Place Victoria, Montreal, Quebec, H4Z 1J7.
(Over 20 subsidiaries of this firm operate in the UK, primary interests including home improvements, bedroom fitments, packaged tours and holidays)

Inco Ltd,
PO Box 44, Royal Trust Tower, Toronto-Dominion Centre, Toronto, Ontario, M5K 1N4.
(Around 20 operations in the UK, usually under the general business name 'Inco Engineered Products Ltd)

Lawson Mardon Group Ltd,
Suite 401, 6711 Mississanga Road, Mississange, Ontario, LSN 2W3.
(Around 40 operations in the UK, mainly involved in the production of plastic packaging materials)

Petro-Canada,
PO Box 2844, Calgary, Alberta, T2P 3E3.
(30 plus operations currently exist in the United Kingdom)

The Royal Bank of Canada,
1 Place Ville Marie, Montreal, Quebec, H3C 3AG.
(Many branches of this firm operate in the United Kingdom, a significant proportion in the Isle of Man and Guernsey)

The Seagram Company Ltd,
1430 Peel Street, Montreal, Quebec, H3A 1S9.
(Distilling operations in the United Kingdom are far too numerous to mention, running literally into hundreds, and including such names as 'Morgan Rum', 'Glenlivet Distillers' and 'House of Seagram')

Trion Financial Corporation,
PO Box 48, Commerce Court Postal Station, Toronto Dominion
    Centre, Toronto, Ontario, M5L 1B7.
(Numerous operations exist in the United Kingdom, mostly under
the general trading names 'RTC Holdings Co' and 'Royal Trust
Asset Management Holdings (UK) Ltd)

Hiram-Walker-Gooderham & Worts Ltd.,
Box 2518, Walkerville, 2072 Riverside Road East, Windsor,
    Ontario, N8Y 4S5.
(A subsidiary of UK company Allied-Lyons Plc, this particular
firm has 30 plus distilling operations located in various parts of the
United Kingdom)

B.   Major UK Companies with Bases or Subsidiaries in Canada

    * Brackets indicate the name under which the firm or organisation
trades in Canada.

A F Bulgin & Co Plc,
Bypass Road, Barking, Essex, IG11 OAZ.
Oil, gas and energy.
(Cirkit Enterprises Ltd)

Amec Plc.,
Sandiway House, Northwich, Cheshire, CW8 2YA.
Property Holdings, fire protection and electricity products and
services.
(William Press and Son (Canada) Ltd)

Airclaims Group Ltd,
Cardinal Point, Newall Road, Heathrow Airport, Hounslow,
    Middlesex, TW6 2AS.
(Airclaims Specialists of Canada)

Airship Industries Ltd,
Bond House, 347-353 Chiswick High Road, London, W4 4HS.
(LTA Systems Inc)

Allied Colloids Group Plc,
Cleckheaton Road, Low Moor, Bradford, W Yorks, BD12 OJZ.
(Allied Colloids (Canada) Inc)

Allied-Lyons Plc,
Allied House, 156 St. John Street, London, EC1P 1AR.

Amersham International Plc,
Amersham Place, Little Chalfont, Buckinghamshire, HP7 9NA.
(Amersham Canada Ltd)

Andola Fibres Ltd,
Springhead Mills, Oakworth, Keighley, West Yorks, BD22 7RX.
(Andola Fibres (Canada) Ltd)

Applied Holographics Plc,
Braxted Park, Witham, Essex, CM8 3XB.
(A H Corp)

Laura Ashley Holdings Plc,
Carno, Caersws, Powys, SY17 5LQ.
(Laura Ashley Shops Ltd)

B A T Industries Plc,
Windsor House, 50 Victoria Street, London, SW1H ONL.
(Scottish Pulp Canada Ltd, Imasco Ltd, V G Instruments Canada Inc)

BICC Plc,
Devonshire House, Mayfair Place, London, W1X 5FH.
(BICC Canada Inc, BICC Canada Holdings Inc, Balfour Beatty (Canada) Ltd, Phillips Cables Ltd)

J C Bamford Excavators Ltd,
Rocester, Uttoxeter, Staffs, SRT14 5JP.
(JCB Excavators Ltd)

Bass Plc,
30 Portland Place, London, W1N 3DF.
(Bass Investment (Canada) Ltd, Commonwealth Hospitality Ltd)

Brent Chemicals International Plc,
Ridgeway, Iver, Bucks, SLO 9JJ.

British Aerospace,
11 Strand, London, WC2N 5JT.
(British Aerospace Canada Ltd)

British Gas Plc,
Rivermill House, 152 Grosvenor Road, London, SW1V 3JL.
(British Gas (Canada) Ltd)

The British Petroleum Co. Ltd,
Britannic House, Moor Lane, London, EC24 9BU.
(Hendrix Nutrition Canada Ltd, BP Canadian Holdings Ltd, BP Nova Scotia (Exploration), Aquatess Ltd)

British Steel Plc,
9 Albert Embankment, London, SE1 7SN.
(British Steel Canada Inc, Normines Inc)

British Telecommunication Plc,
81 Newgate Street, London, EC1A 7AJ.
(BT (Canada) Holdings Inc, British Telecom (Canada)
Investments Inc, CTG Inc, Mitel Corp)

The Burmah Oil Plc,
Burmah House, Pipers Way, Swindon, Wilts, SN3 1RE.
(Dussek Campbell Ltd, Expandite (Canada) Ltd)

Cadbury Schweppes Plc,
1-4 Connaught Place, London, W2 2EX.
(Cadbury Schweppes Canada Inc, Canada Dry Inc, Fry-Cadbury
(1971) Ltd)

Central Electricity Generating Board,
Sudbury House, 15 Newgate Street, London, EC1A 7AU.
(Canada Electricity Generating Board Exploration (Canada) Ltd)

Century Oils Group Plc,
PO Box 2, Century Street, Hanley, Stoke-on-Trent, ST1 5HU.
(Century Oils (Canada) Ltd)

Coats Viyella Plc,
Bank House, Charlotte Street, Manchester, M1 4ET.
(J & P Coats (Canada) Inc, Patons & Baldwins Canada Inc, Jaeger
(Canada) Inc)

Costain Group Plc,
111 Westminster Bridge Road, London, SE1 7UE.
(Western Lane and Marine Pipelines Ltd, Petrocarbon
Developments Corporation, Costain Concrete Tie Co. Ltd)

Daily Mail and General Trust Plc,
(Newspapers and Publications), New Carmelite House, London,
  EC4Y OJA.
(Bouverie Holdings Inc, Bouverie Investments Ltd, Harmsworth
Holdings Ltd)

Fisons Plc,
Fison House, Princes Street, Ipswich, IP1 1QH.
(ARL Applied Research Laboratories Ltd, Chibiluma Sales Ltd,
Fisons Corp Ltd, Fisons Horticulture Inc, Fisons Instruments Ltd)

GEC Plessey Telecommunication Holdings Ltd,
PO Box 53, Telephone Road, Coventry, W. Midlands, CV4 1HJ.
(GEC Plessey Telecommunications (Canada) Ltd)

The Genereal Electric Company Plc,
1 Stanhope Gate, London, W1A 1EH.
(Various firms operating in Canada)

Granada Group Plc,
36 Golden Square, London, W1R 4AH.
(DPCE Computer Services Inc, Granada Distribution (Canada) Ltd, Granada TV Rental Ltd, Steristystems Inc)

Grand Metropolitan Plc,
11/12 Hanover Square, London, W1A 1DP.
(Express Dairy Co. of Canada Ltd, Palliser Distillers Ltd, IDV Wines and Spirits Inc)

Hawker Siddeley Group Plc,
18 St. James Square, London, SW1Y 4LJ.
(Operates in Canada under various business names)

Imperial Chemical Industries Plc,
Imperial Chemical House, Millbank, London, SW1P 3JF.
(Imperial Chemical Industries of Canada Ltd)

Ladbroke Group Plc,
Chancel House, Neasden Lane, London, NW10 2XE.
(162371 Canada Inc, 163949 Canada Inc)

Lucas Industries Plc,
Great King Street, Birmingham, B19 2XF.
(Lucas Aerospace Inc, Cole Motion Inc)

E D & F Man Ltd,
Sugar Quay, Lower Thames Street, London, EC3R 6DU.
(Man Sugar Inc)

Marks and Spencer Plc,
Michael House, Baker Street, London, W1A 1DN.
(Marks & Spencer Holdings Canada Inc, Marks & Spencer Canada Inc)

Racal Electronics Plc,
Western Road, Bracknell, Berkshire, RG12 1RG.
(Operates several business enterprises, in the sectors of musical records, security systems, and various electronics industries)

Saatchi & Saatchi Co Plc,
15 Lower Regent Street, London, SW1Y 4LR.
(Ted Bates Advertising Ltd, Saatchi & Saatchi Canada Inc, and various other business names)

W H Smith Group Plc,
Strand House, 7 Holbein Place, London, SW1W 8NR.
(W H Smith Canada Ltd)

Taylor Woodrow Plc,
10 Park Street, London, W1Y 4DD.
(Monarch Development Corp, Taylor Woodrow of Canada Ltd,
etc)

Thorn EMI Plc,
4 Tenterden Street, Hanover Square, London, W1A 2AY.
(EPSCAN Consultants Ltd, THORN EMI (Canada) Ltd, Thorn
TV Rentals Canada Ltd)

Unigate Plc,
Unigate House, Blackfriars, London, EC4P 4BQ.
(Biocon Canada Inc, Unilever Canada Ltd)

United Biscuits Holdings Plc,
Grant House, PO Box 40, Syon Lane, Isleworth, Middlesex, TW7
5NN.
(United Biscuits Holdings (Canada) Ltd)

British Banks with Companies and Subsidiaries in Canada

Barclays Plc,
54 Lombard Street, London, EC3P 3AH.
(Barclays Bank of Canada)

Lloyds Bank Plc,
71 Lombard Street, London, EC3P 3BS.
(Lloyds Bank Canada, Lloyds Bank Canada Leasing Corp, Lloyds
Bank Canada Mortgage Corp, Lloyds Bank Financial Corp)

National Westminster Bank Plc,
41 Lothbury, London, EC2P 2BP.
(National Westminster Bank)

Insurance Firms with Companies and Subsidiaries in Canada

Commercial Union Assurance Co. Ltd,
St Helens, 1 Undershaft, London, EC3P 3DQ.
(Commercial Union of Canada Holdings Ltd)

Legal and General Group Plc,
Temple Court, 11 Queen Victoria Street, London, EC4N 4TP.
(Victoria Reinsurance Management Canada Ltd)

Friends' Provident Life Office,
Pixham End, Dorking, Surrey, RH4 1QA.
(Over 12 different operations in Canada)

CHAPTER FIVE

Living in Canada

General Advice

Culture shock is not something that normally presents itself regularly to the migrant to Canada, where life styles are not too dissimilar to those with which the Briton is usually familiar. Those sometimes disabling symptoms of failure to acclimatise to life in many other parts of the world: alienation; inability to cope with nationals' beliefs and traditions; total feelings of isolation, rejection and sometimes repulsion, are rarely ever experienced by the British migrant to Canada, who might instead suffer the less traumatic symptoms of homesickness, mild doubts and uncertainties, worries over house hunting, and generally coming to terms with life in this new and exciting land.

The ease with which one fits into Canadian society will of course vary from one province to the next, more so when one takes into account regional differences in terms of language preferences, climatic variations, density of population, and so on.

But, at the risk of repeating something pointed out many times already in 'Live and work in Canada', it must be reiterated that once having made their move the overwhelming majority of Canada-bound Britons have very few if any regrets. Higher living standards, better environment, and majestic scenery, once experienced totally obliterate whatever doubts, uncertainties and homesickness the newcomer once fell prey to.

The French Language

Though not essential to making oneself understood in almost whatever part of Canada their travels take them, there will be times

149

when some knowledge of French will prove invaluable, even if only to fend off potential hostility and possible alienation from those citizens fiercely proud of this as their native tongue (some speak nothing but French, even though in truth the vast majority of Canadians are bilingual). To make matters just a little more complicated, in many instances their variation of French often differs dramatically to that spoken in their 'native' country, France.

That need to at least familiarise oneself with a few words of French will become more apparent in such as Quebec, with its ongoing issue of separatism, that is a demand for Quebec to be recognised as unilaterally French.

Do I Need to Learn French?

As already considered, though not essential in most parts of Canada where even those who prefer to use their French tongues usually have the additional benefits of bilingual speech, there are times when at least a working knowledge of French will prove highly useful to the migrant and tourist alike. We mustn't forget the fact that a little courtesy towards nationals, such as attempting to communicate with them in their chosen language, will go a great way towards the newcomers' integration into Canadian society.

Much of course depends upon the intended duration of the visit to Canada; if for a working holiday or but a year or so seconded by one's employing firm, that need to learn anything but a modicum of French is far less important than is undoubtedly the case for those who intend to spend the rest of their lives in Canada. If that new home is one in the French-speaking quarters of Canada, then learning French is not advisable – it is an absolute essential!

In business circles, particularly in the field of international trade, English is the prime language of industry and commerce.

Learning French

French is not a difficult language to learn, given that countless French words have entered the English language through many centuries, hardly any of them unchanged in the course of time, but a great many of them recognisable in whatever form they take. 'Le Cigarette' (French) for instance, is instantly recognisable as 'The Cigarette' to which the non-French speaking Britain would refer. Amongst other everyday words to take on such a familiar note are, English first, French alternative follows: Table: Table; Synonym: Synonyme; September: Septembre; Householder (Occupant): Occupant(e).

The one major problem usually encountered in learning the

French language is that of 'gender', namely a method of according nouns status as either male (prefixed 'le'), or female (prefixed 'la'). But given that we 'forgive' pigeon English from whatever national it emanates, there is little or nothing to worry about over this concept of gender; one day it will all fall naturally into place.

There are several methods by which to learn French, whether from within Britain or once the migrant settles down in his or her new homeland.

Amongst the primary methods of learning French are:

Local Authority and Further Education Classes

There must surely be no college of further education in which basic or higher grade French does not feature in that curriculum available to full or part-time students, sometimes on a day basis, at other time by attendance at evening classes.

Courses are usually offered at basic, intermediate and advanced level, many of them leading to appropriate qualifications – optional of course! In most colleges basic conversational language courses are available, usually with students conversing with one another entirely in French – very useful practice indeed, even if a little awe-inspiring in the early stages.

Interested individuals should consult their local colleges of further education, or else contact local education departments of nearby education authorities for information of exactly what is available in their area.

Courses range from very inexpensive, to in some cases entirely free of charge. Some problems might exist in that many courses begin at the commencement of normal education terms, in which case one might be placed at a distinct disadvantage if attempting to join a suitable course mid-term. Given however that it is for your own sake you join such a course, and considering also that you might find yourself unable to sit whatever examinations might be available to course members, that mid-term entry need present very few insurmountable difficulties to the course recruit, and in many cases course tutors will allow the individual to 'sit in' on lectures purely to listen and learn from the proceedings without necessarily having to take part in debates or homework and class assignments.

Private Language Schools

Given Britain's entry to Europe, a whole host of private schools have emerged to cater for those wishing to learn the language of other member states. Consequently, French features significantly in those schools, details of which are available under the heading 'Language Schools' in 'Yellow Pages'.

One leading language school with branches throughout Britain is:

Berlitz School of Languages,
79 Wells Street, London, W1A 3BZ.

A list of residential language courses in the United Kingdom is available from:

The National Institute of Adult Continuing Education,
19b De Montfort Street, Leicester, KE1 7GE. 0533 551451

Self Study and Correspondence

Books, Training manuals, tapes, even videos and one-to-one correspondence courses fall within this category. Prices quite naturally vary quite considerably, depending upon what level of training is involved, what personal contact one has with suppliers and tutors, whether books are of the everyday phrase book variety or whether instead they comprise a full range of graded lectures often with cassettes provided as an invaluable back up aid to lessons.

Advertisements for very many highly reputable firms and publishers appear daily in national newspapers and in many other weekly, monthly and other periodic publications. In some book shops, particularly those in larger towns and cities, complete language training courses, usually comprising manual and audio cassettes, are available at usually not too high a cost.

Amongst the many courses and training packages available are those produced by the following firms:

BBC Books,
80 Wood Lane, London, W12 OTT. 081 576 2536

Linguaphone,
St Giles House, 50 Poland Street, London, W1V 4AX. 071 734 0574

Teach Yourself Books, Hodder and Stoughton Educational,
Mill Road, Dunton Green, Sevenoaks, Kent, TN13 2YA. 0732 450111

Routledge,
(The Colloquial Language series), 11 New Fetter Lane, London, EC4P 4EE. 071 583 9855

Language Learning Holidays

Not always a practical alternative for those with jobs or families to care for in Britain, but a very, very good way indeed in which to learn French literally 'as it is spoken'. Working holidays can last for but a few weeks or several months, and can involve a wide range of disciplines by which one might earn one's living while learning that language of the country in which the 'holiday' takes place.

Literally hundreds of opportunities for working holidays are available; as such a representative listing is well outside the scope of this book. The publisher of 'Live and Work in Canada' can provide details of an invaluable guide to those wishing to take advantage of working holidays in all parts of the world, many such opportunities available for those intending to visit France for the purposes of learning the native language.

Details of 'Worldwide Working Holidays' is available on request from:

Grant Dawson Travel,
7 Rockland Road, Putney, London, SW15 2LN.

Courses in Canada

Again available at most colleges of further education, one will find details of all such courses listed in local telephone directories.

Depending upon the length of one's intended visit, as well as destination, it might well be appropriate to leave all language learning until arrival on Canadian soil, with very little but a French phrase book and English-French dictionary by which to provide assistance in potential emergency situations.

But given that French is a fairly easy language to learn, the traveller might best be advised to acquire at least a working knowledge of French from whatever of the earlier options might prove more convenient.

Travelling to Canada

Most people choose to fly to Canada, then continue their journey by bus, train, car or plane. Most international airlines service major Canadian centres, notably Toronto, Montreal and Vancouver.

Amongst main airlines operating direct and indirect services between Britain and Canada are: Air France, Air Canada, CP, Alitalia, British Airways, El Al, KLM, Lufthansa, Scandinavian Airlines and Swissair. Many US airlines operate services between Canada and most other parts of the world.

The major international airlines are **Air Canada** and **Canadian Airlines International**.

Major airports operating international services in Canada are those of: Calgary, Edmonton, Gander, Goose Bay, Halifax, St. John's, Montreal, Ottawa, Toronto, Vancouver and Winnipeg. Most of these airports provide a wide range of additional services to travellers, including foreign exchange, coin-operated lockers, telephones, duty-free shops, news stands and book stores, drugstores, shopping areas, and many also have their own hotel complexes or are within easy reach of high class accommodation facilities.

Around all major airports are provided a wide range of transportation services including bus, taxi and limousine. In addition most reputable car rental firms have offices based in or near main airports.

For Further Information

Scheduled Transatlantic Airlines

Air Canada,
7-8 Conduit Street, London, W1R 9TG.
Telephone:
081 759 2636 (for reservations made from inside London)
0800 181313 (for reservations made from outside of London)
Fax: 071 465 0095
Offer direct flights with frequent services from Heathrow
(London), to Toronto, Montreal, Halifax, St. John's, Calgary,
Edmonton and Vancouver.
Fares vary significantly depending upon class of travel, reservation period, standby bookings, and so on.

Air India,
17-18 New Bond Street, London, W1Y OBD. Tel: 071 491 7979.
  Fax: 071 493 4050
Direct flights between Heathrow and Toronto. Flights usually available only on Tuesdays and Fridays.

British Airways,
156 Regent Street, London, W1R 5TA.
Telephone:
London: 081 897 4000
Glasgow: 041 332 9666
Manchester: 061 228 6311
Flights direct from London to Montreal, Vancouver and Toronto.

Canadian Airlines International,
Rothschild House, Whitgift Centre, Croydon, Surrey, CR9 3HN.
Telephone:
081 667 0666 (for reservations made from within London)

0345 616 767 (for reservations made from outside London)
Fax: 081 688 2997
Provides regular flights from London and Manchester direct to
Toronto, Ottawa, Calgary, Edmonton and Vancouver.

Air Charter Companies

ASAT
Tel: 0737 778560
Departures from Gatwick and Stanstead direct to Toronto and
Vancouver.

Falcon
Tel: 071 221 0088
Flights from Gatwick, Birmingham and Manchester direct to
Toronto and Vancouver.

Globespan
Tel: 0293 541541
Direct flights from 10 UK airports to 6 Canadian destinations.

Getting There by Sea

A great many services offer transportation of passengers and
goods. All travel agencies will provide full details of those services
available. Amongst major shipping lines operating in Canada are:

Canberra Cruises Ltd,
3080 Younge Street, Suite 4000, Toronto, Ontario, M4R 3NI.

Freighter Cruise Service,
Suite 103, 5929 Monkland Avenue, Montreal, Quebec.

Polish Ocean Lines,
McLean Kennedy Inc, 410 St. Nicolas Street, Passenger
  Department, Montreal, H2Y 2P5.

British-based offices of shipping lines offering services to Canada
include the following:

Blue Star Line,
34-35 Leadenhall Street, London, EC3A 1AR.

Gdynia America Shipping Lines Ltd.,
238 City Road, London, EC1V 2QL.

Royal Viking Line,
3 Vere Street, London, W1M 9HQ.

Travelling in Canada

So vast a country, Canada also has widely scattered population centres often with enormous distances separating them. Not surprisingly air transportation assumes vital importance for domestic transportation of goods and passengers.

Travel by road also proves popular for domestic transportation, and particularly in rural areas car ownership is a must. Over 75% of Canadian households own at least one car. Here there are more road miles per person than in any other part of the world except Australia.

More detailed information regarding travelling in Canada is available from:

Canadian Government Office of Tourism,
Department of Industry, Trade and Commerce, 235 Queen Street, Ottawa, Ontario, KIA OH5.

Travelling by Air

Three major airlines operate on domestic routes: Air Canada, Canadian Airlines International and Wardair. Canadian Airways International operate a domestic network covering over 160 Canadian cities.

Internal air fares are high, though reductions can be obtained by purchasing VUSA tickets. Many airlines offer discounts to seasonal and longer-term ticket holders.

Various cut rates apply to students, and those willing to fly on standby arrangements.

Domestic services link major towns and cities with even the remotest areas, though quite naturally for economic reasons, such services might be limited to but a few flights each week.

Even the sparsely populated Maritime regions are well serviced with regular flights between Toronto/Montreal and Halifax being provided by Air Canada, Canadian Airlines and Air Nova. Though Halifax's airport is located some 26 miles or so from the city, the airport provides a regular limousine service from the city centre for a nominal fee at the time of writing amounting to $8.

Toronto's main airport is the Lester B Pearson International Airport, named after the 1960s Nobel Peace Prize-winning Prime Minister of Canada. The airport, located some 18 miles from the centre of the city, is linked by regular express airport buses operated by Gray Coaches.

Low cost domestic flights from Toronto are provided by:

Travel CUTS,
187 College Street, Toronto.

Useful Addresses and Information

The main British office of **Canadian Airlines** is:

62 Trafalgar Square, London, WC2N 5EW. 071 930 3501

Canadian Airlines International have offices based at:

2500 Four Rentall Centre, 1055 Dunsmuir Street, Box 49370, Vancouver, British Columbia, V7X 1R9

Private plane licences and essential information is obtainable from:

Transport Canada,
SLPP, Ottawa, Ontario, Canada, K1A ON5.

Travelling by Rail

Major passenger rail service Via Rail operates alongside various regional services, for instance BC Rail and Ontario Northland. Via Rail operates even in sparsely populated areas, and consequently is heavily reliant upon government subsidies, particularly for those services operating on long-distance networks. Rail travel of the future, particularly that operated by Via Rail, is set to offer a far speedier trip to its passengers, with VR's plans for 'space age' LRC trains; that LRC incidentally is the acronym for the intended form the transportation will offer as Light, Rapid and Comfortable. The introduction of these trains of tomorrow is set to compete favourably with the speed of air transportation, at a fraction of the cost involved to passengers.

VIA Rail offices located throughout the country, provide cut price travel to holders of 'Canrailpasses', the cost for which is determined by the age of the applicant and the rail network upon which he or she intends to journey. Passes are available for varying periods of time, and cover specific regional networks or nationwide transportation.

In so large a country, one might at least for the present, assume that air transportation is the only option for those wishing to travel from one centre to a destination many thousands of miles removed. And for those more in tune with life in the fast lane, this will no doubt be the case. But for those for whom spectacular scenery and the privilege of glimpsing wildlife roaming as nature intended, nothing will suffice for that 3-day plus rail journey from Toronto to Vancouver. Much the same could be said for those railway networks operating on routes through the Rockies, though not perhaps for the far less interesting journey through miles and miles of unrelenting and feature-free prairie lands.

Types of Train

High-speed trains link most major towns and cities; in outlying areas the traveller might take advantage of the magnificent scenery available from the windows of slower, perhaps older forms of transportation; but in all places standards of rail travel are high and come with the added benefits of a proven 'track' record on safety standards.

In major cities, primarily Toronto, speedy commuter trains 'GO Trains' an acronym for 'Government Of Toronto', transport the traveller direct to the heart of the city from even the farthest reaching parts of Toronto.

All long-distance trains have sleeping accommodation, buffet cars and restaurants, not surprisingly really when you consider that journeys might last for several days. So comfortable can be the journey through some of the world's most scenic and breathtakingly beautiful parts, that many tourist trains operate, offering a virtual holiday on rails.

Timetables

All travel agencies, tourist offices, railway stations and rail lines, can provide detailed timetables, usually on a provincial level. VIA Rail, operating services throughout the entire country, has offices in all major towns and cities, and can provide nationwide timetables.

Reservations and obtaining of tickets follows a procedure very much similar to that with which we are familiar in Britain. Tickets can be obtained and reservations made in advance, either in person or by telephone. Standby services differ between railway companies; both periods of notice and reduced terms being offered can vary not only between companies but also between provinces. All such information is available from whatever source timetables are obtained.

Reservation of seats is a rare occurrence in sparsely populated areas of Canada, but a distinct advantage in major towns and cities, and particularly where one's journey takes place between main centres.

That problem of how much knowledge of French one might require in obtaining tickets in such as Quebec need not cause undue concern, since as said so many times in 'Live and Work in Canada', most Canadians are bilingual. If however you wish to avoid whatever problems might exist should one come face-to-face with a belligerent – and there are few of them – 'French-speaking' rail official or ticket office clerk, that French phrase book will prove invaluable for whatever few words one requires to obtain that ticket.

Making the Journey

Again, the journey will prove very much similar to that with which travellers by British Rail are familiar. Reserved seats will be indicated not only on your ticket but also on the seat itself; varying 'classes' of transportation are available; ticket inspections will take place either on the train or upon arrival at one's destination.

Useful Information

VIA Rail is represented in the UK by:

Compass Travel,
PO Box 113, Peterborough, PE1 1LE. Tel: 0733 51780.
  Fax: 0733 892601

Thistle Air,
22 Bank Street, Kilmarnock, KA1 1HG. Tel: 0563 31121.
  Fax: 0563 37679

Travelling by Coach

Not surprisingly in the world's largest country, hundreds of bus and coach services operate, many of them confining their services to western regions. Greyhound Lines of Canada provide the greatest number of services and most extensive networks. In eastern areas one finds countless regional services, many of them operating on a provincial basis.

Greyhound buses operate throughout Canada, offering discounts based on 7-day, 15-day or 30-day 'Ameripass' tickets.

Coaches offer inexpensive and extremely comfortable transportation, usually with air conditioning, on-board toilet facilities, and sometimes video entertainment provided on longer routes.

Major bus lines are as follows:

Greyhound Lines of Canada Ltd.,
877 Greyhound Way SW, Calgary, Alberta, T3C 3V8.

Greyhound Inc.,
901 Main Street, Suite 2500, Dallas, Texas 75202, USA.

Voyageur Colonial Ltd.,
265 Catherine Street, Ottawa, Ontario, K1R 7S5.

A very useful document 'The Official Bus Guide' is available from:

Russell's Guides Inc.,
PO Box 278, Cedar Rapids, Iowa 52406.

Useful Information

Greyhound World Travel has a UK office located as follows:

Greyhound World Travel Ltd.,
Sussex House, London Road, East Grinstead, West Sussex, RH19 1LD. Tel: 0342 317317. Fax: 0342 328519

Travelling by Sea

Coastal transportation whether for practical or tourist and sightseeing purposes is available in most parts of Canada. Details are available from all main tourist offices and travel agencies.

Nautical maps can be obtained from:

Canadian Hydrographic Servec,
Department of Fisheries and Oceans, Ottawa, Ontario, Canada, KIA OE6.

Travelling by Ferry

Ferry systems operate in most parts of Canada, usually with main companies restricting their services to Western or Eastern regions.

In western areas, there are frequent daily ferry services between Vancouver to Victoria and the Gulf Islands, for a journey lasting around 2½ hours. Other services operate between islands, not always on a daily basis, and sometimes offering journeys that can last for up to 15 hours in each direction.

In western areas the main ferry company is:

British Columbia Ferry Corporation,
1112 Fort Street, Victoria, British Columbia, Canada, V8V 4V2. Tel: 604 669 1211. Fax: 604 381 5452

A wide variety of ferry services operate between the many scattered islands of Canada's eastern parts. Some services operate only in the summer, many of them on a toll-free basis. Prince Edward Island and Nova Scotia are linked to New Brunswick by a year-round car ferry service.

One of several ferry companies operating in western areas is:

Lion Ferry,
Portland Ltd., International Terminal, Portland, Maine, USA. 207 755 5616

Public Transport in Towns and Cities

Excellent transport facilities operate in all major centres, though as one might expect services and standards are somewhat limited in remote parts. Details of transport facilities are available from all local tourist offices; almost all towns and cities, even the smaller ones, have at least one such office available to provide travel brochures, timetables, and details regarding fees and method of obtaining tickets.

The reader should refer to that section 'City by City, Region by Region' earlier in this book, for details of major provincial and territorial tourist offices.

Travelling by Taxi

Taxi services operate throughout, providing a safe and reliable form of transportation in all parts of the country. In more remote, snow-bound areas, transportation is usually by means of four-wheel heavy-duty vehicles; far less elegant than the limousines that might transport one between city centres and airports, but given the rough terrain to which they are ideally suited, they do at least provide as safe a form of transport as is possible to come by.

In Toronto, one of the largest taxi companies is Metro Cab, with almost 1,000 vehicles plying for custom on the busy streets. Many other companies are available to the traveller, who will find details listed in the city's 'Yellow Pages'.

Amongst major taxi companies of British Columbia are Blue Bird, Empress, Vancouver Island Transit and B.C. Hydro.

Travelling by Subway

Toronto and Montreal have extensive and highly efficient underground subway systems. In Toronto, lines run below the main streets Yongue and Bloor, forming a crosswork system of lines and stop-off points all operating essentially from one main station. Usually services operate from 6am to 1am.

In Montreal a superb Metro system is provided by the Montreal Urban Community Transport Commission (MUCTC).

Street Cars

In Toronto street cars offer a form of travel that many Britons have long forgotten. Similar to trams that operate still in some parts of Britain, electric street cars came to Toronto in the late 19th century, but unlike that similar system allowed to fall into disuse in Britain, Toronto's cars prove highly popular with residents and newcomers alike.

Car Rental

The reader's attention is drawn to the next main section 'Cars and Driving' for details of car rental facilities available throughout Canada. Rates, rental conditions, minimum driving age, all vary provincially. The driver should therefore make certain that in hiring a car in one province for intended journeys into another, that he or she might not inadvertently break some rule which might invalidate his or her insurance on the vehicle concerned.

All car rental firms are listed in local telephone directories, with details also available from tourist and travel information centres.

Travelling by Bus

Excellent bus services operate in all accessible parts of the country, with better services quite naturally being offered in more densely populated towns and cities.

Gray Coach and Greyhound operate widespread networks; other smaller firms operate on a local, usually provincial basis.

Toronto's bus terminal on Bay Street is the busiest in Canada, and is currently being re-designed and altered to cope with increased demand and a heavy flow of passengers. In downtown Toronto trolley buses are a frequent sight, powered by overhead electric cables, and providing a very inexpensive mode of transportation.

Quality and safety standards are high, cost of travel relatively inexpensive, making for a form of transportation that proves extremely popular with nationals and newcomers to Canada.

In the less densely populated Maritime regions, Greyhound Coaches, noted for their almost universal availability, do not operate any services at all. Local tourist offices will advise the newcomer on what services are available in outlying areas.

When travelling by bus one is usually required to tender the exact fare for the journey since bus drivers do not normally carry change.

Cars and Driving

Cars are not so much luxury items in Canada – they are absolutely essential, particularly in rural areas. In sparsely populated areas, and in such as the Maritime and Northland regions, transportation is almost one hundred per cent dependent upon the car.

Your Driving Licence

Foreign driving licences are valid in Canada, subject as for most things to regional (provincial) variations. In the Yukon for instance, the Briton may drive with a UK licence for up to 30 days, whilst a similar licence will cover a period of up to six months in British Columbia. On average though, the British driving licence is valid for a period of up to 3 months. Those visiting Canada for longer periods, perhaps for indeterminate duration, should apply for an international driving permit.

An International Driving Permit must be accompanied at all times by the driver's national driving licence.

Taking Your Car to Canada

For those intending to settle in Canada for a year or more, their vehicles will be regarded by the Vehicle Licensing Centre as a 'permanent export' and should therefore have registration documents returned to the Vehicle Licensing Centre in Swansea, or else appropriate documents completed and delivered to Canadian Licensing Authorities. Strict laws apply in Canada regarding exhaust emissions, and those cars that do not meet appropriate requirements regarding filtering of fumes will not be passed for use on Canada's roads.

You might of course check with British Licensing authorities and insurance companies regarding any refunds of tax or insurance premiums to which you might be entitled.

One very important point to take into consideration in deciding whether or not to take your current car abroad with you is the fact that Canadians drive on the right-hand side of the road; unless you have a particular affinity with a vehicle designed for driving on the left, then it might be more pertinent to consider either leaving your present car behind if your visit to Canada is one of intended short duration, or else purchasing a suitable vehicle from within Canada where that stay is one of a potentially indeterminate period.

Buying a Car in Canada

Though purchasing a car in Canada is fraught with the same potential difficulties facing motorists in other parts of the world, it is generally advisable particularly when buying an older vehicle to opt for one possessing a Safety Standards Certificate. This certificate indicates that the vehicle has been inspected by a licensed operator and should be free of major defects and potential threats to safety. The inspection however does not include the engine, transmission and a few other parts.

Those problems one might face if purchasing a car on which the previous 'owner' still owes substantial amounts to a loan company, might be avoided by checking on whether any 'liens' are registered against the vehicle concerned. A lien is an indication of a loan being taken out with the vehicle concerned being used as security, as well as proof that the person purporting to be outright owner does in fact exist in that capacity.

Checks on vehicle ownership required to protect your own interests may be made by contact with your local Personal Property Registration Offices, branches for which organisation operate in Ontario and other provincial capitals. Though the check takes a day to complete and a fee is required for the service, this should be viewed as a small price to pay for the assurance that one's newly acquired vehicle is not likely to be repossessed to cover the outstanding debts of others.

Registering a vehicle takes place at local Vehicle Licensing Offices, details of which are provided in the blue pages of telephone directories. Documentation required to register ownership include the vehicle permit (signed by both buyer and seller), Safety Standards Certificate, and bill of sale showing the purchase price.

Upon sale of a vehicle the previous owner removes and retains possession of vehicle plates; the new owner receives alternative plates after licensing has been completed, unless he or she already possesses plates from a vehicle owned previously.

Though one can register without the Safety Standards Certificate, it will not be permissible to drive the car or be provided with plates for the vehicle until the vehicle has been certified as safe and a certificate obtained.

Cost of Purchase

A survey conducted by 'Canada News' in 1991, showed the following average prices for 'nearly new' cars as advertised in a wide representative sample of Canadian newspapers.

Ford Escort	$8,799
Ford Topaz	$8,888
Nissan Sentra DLX	$11,390
Honda Civic	$14,155
Honda Accord	$15,495
BMW 318i	$23,271

The Canadian Automobile Association offers much useful information regarding new and used car prices, in its annual guide 'Autopinion'.

Generally however, one finds very little of financial benefit to result from taking one's current vehicle abroad, given that new and used vehicle prices are often far more competitive than those for purchases made in Britain. One must however consider the condition of used cars in relation to Canada's harsh weather; salted roads might lead to a great degree of chassis corrosion. Rough terrain in many parts will doubtless have a similar adverse effect upon the condition of even 'nearly new' vehicles. Always have a full inspection made on used cars before making that vitally important decision of whether or not to purchase.

Running a Car

Petrol, sold by the litre, comes at widely differing prices across Canada, sometimes prices are as much as doubled from one source to the next.

Car servicing presents little problem in almost all parts of the country. Amongst specialist services offered by garages in most towns and cities are those for cars originating from Britain, Japan, Europe and North America.

All provinces require that drivers take out liability for bodily injury or death, and damage to the property of others. Visiting drivers must therefore take out full liability insurance, the cover for which varies between provinces. Full details regarding insurance, with much other useful information thrown in for good measure is available from:

The Insurance Bureau of Canada,
181 University Avenue, Toronto, Ontario, Canada, M5H 3M7.
416 362 2031

The Canadian Automobile Association,
1775 Courtwood Crescent, Ottawa, K2C 3J2.
This latter organisation is closely connected to the AA and RAC.

Motorists intending to take their own vehicles to Canada may experience some difficulty in arranging adequate insurance before leaving their own country. They should therefore contact an insurance broker immediately upon entry to Canada, where they will discover that written evidence of claim-free driving in recent years will greatly reduce their premiums.

Car Rental

Amongst larger car rental firms operating throughout are Tilden, Budget, Hertz, Thrifty, Rent-a-Wreck and Avis. Though rates for some firms might be standard throughout the continent, remember that provincial taxes may have a significant impact upon car hire charges between provinces.

Car rental firms operate in all major cities and from outside of airports and seaports. Most companies will not rent cars to under-21 year olds (sometimes this minimum age is extended to 25 years), and usually not without an accepted credit card being presented for payment, or alternatively a hefty cash deposit. Usually one is also required to prove possession of a valid passport and return airline ticket.

The majority of hire cars drive on unleaded petrol.

Insurance requirements must cover public liability and damage to property. Most, particularly the large rental firms, will waive collision damage and personal accident insurance at an additional charge.

At the time of writing, car rental rates vary from £115 a week, depending upon the size of the car and whether unlimited kilometrage, or mileage, is available. Some firms offer several hundred kilometres free or else charge a daily rate with an additional charge being made for distance travelled.

Several British offices will handle reservations on behalf of those intending to visit Canada. Included amongst them are:

Avis Rent-a-Car Systems Inc.,
Avis House, Park Road, Bracknell, Berkshire, RG12 2DS. 0344 426644

Bricar International Car Rental Limited,
28/30 Woodcote Road, Wallington, Surrey, SM6 ONN. 081 773 2312

Budget Rent A Car Ltd.,
41 Marlowes, Hemel Hempstead, Herts, HP1 1LD. 0442 232555

Hertz Europe Ltd.,
Hertz House, Bath Road, Cranford, Middlesex, TW5 9SW. 081 759 2499

Thrifty Car Rental,
The Old Court House, Hughenden Road, High Wycombe, Bucks, HP13 5DT. 0494 474767

Tilden Rent A Car (Europcar),
Bushey House, High Street, Bushey, Herts, WD2 1RE. 081 950 4080

Roads

In southern parts, highways are of extremely high standard. In the less traffic-laden roads of northern Canada, roads are often loosely surfaced secondary highways. All roads are clearly signposted by individual provincial highway authorities.

The TransCanada highway traverses the country between St. John's, Newfoundland, Victoria and British Columbia for almost 8,000 kilometres, and is also well signposted throughout all provinces.

Road maps are available from:

Canadian Automobile Association,
1775 Courtwood Court, Ottawa, Ontario, Canada, K2C 3J2.

Driving

Driving takes place on the right hand side of the road.

As for many other rules and regulations to which the national and non-national must comply, those set at provincial level obviously lead to wide variation from one province to the next. Such is the case for many rules of the road.

To illustrate the variations between provinces, the driver might turn right on a red light in all provinces other than Quebec. The minimum driving age in Newfoundland is 17 years; in all other parts one might take to the road at the age of 16. And to demonstrate again the differing rules placed upon motorists in various parts of the country, in Ontario studded tyres are absolutely banned; in the Northwest Territories, The Yukon and Saskatchewan, they are permitted the entire year.

In some provinces and territories it is mandatory that the motorist drives with headlights on for extended periods after dawn and before sunset. In the Yukon, law demands that headlights be on at all times. Throughout Canada, it is against the law to drive with parking lights turned on.

Seat belts must be universally worn by all occupants of the vehicle. Child restraints are mandatory.

Speed limits vary provincially; in built-up areas of Canada the speed limit is 30 mph/50 km/h. One exception to this general rule applies to drivers in Prince Edward Island where the limit is 37 mph/60 km/h.

On main highways, speed limits vary from 50 mph/80 km/h to 62 mph/100 km/h. Speed limits are indicated in kilometres only.

Federal driving laws of course apply throughout. Driving with 0.08% of alcohol in your blood is considered a serious offence no matter the province in which it is committed. If the police believe a driver might be driving whilst under the influence of alcohol, even though no accident or obvious signs are visible, they have the right to stop him or her and carry out a breathalyser test to assess blood alcohol level.

That 0.08% level incidentally is reached by most people having drunk in excess of one bottle of beer (or its alcohol equivalent) within the hour. Penalties for driving whilst impaired by alcohol are severe, as is that for refusing to take a breathalyser test when requested to do so. At the time of writing, first offences range from $50 to $2,000, imprisonment of up to six months – or both!

Petrol, known to Canadians as 'gas' is sold by the litre. The majority of hire-cars drive on unleaded petrol (gas).

Canadian winters do not make for enjoyable driving conditions, other than for those harbouring a burning desire for skid-pan training. Black ice, white-outs, blizzards, snow storms – all are common, and due to the vastly inflated accident rate they produce one often finds even main routes blocked off by the police until the hazard has diminished. Those who do find themselves stranded in unfamiliar territory as a result of severe weather conditions, might be pleased to know that locals are usually well-disposed towards providing room for you in their homes until you may safely continue your journey. Colloquially the recipients of such hospitality are said to be 'Storm-Staying'.

Radio stations maintain a continuous information service for motorists during periods of adverse weather conditions.

Motoring Organisations

Main offices are as follows:

Alberta Motor Association,
11230-110 Street, Edmonton, Alberta.

Canadian Automobile Association,
1175 Courtwood Crescent, Ottawa, Ontario, K2C 3J2.

Canadian Automobile Sports Clubs,
5385 Younge Street, Suite 28, PO Box 97, Willowdale, Ontario, M2N 5S7.

Hamilton Automobile Club,
393 Main Street East, Box 2090, Hamilton, Ontario.

Manitoba Motor League,
870 Empress Street, Box 1400, Winnipeg, Manitoba.

Maritime Automobile Association,
Haymarket Square Shopping Centre, Saint John, New Brunswick.

Ontario Motor League,
2 Carlton Street, Suite 619, Toronto, Canada.

Quebec Automobile Club,
2600 Laurier Blvd, Quebec, PQ.

Saskatchewan Motor Club Ltd.,
200 Albert Street North, Regina, Saskatchewan.

The British Columbia Automobile Association,
PO Box 9900, Vancouver, British Columbia.

Touring Club Montreal,
1425 Rue de la Montagne, Montreal, PQ.

Various motoring organisations including those with which we are familiar in Britain, are affiliated to the Canadian Automobile Association and its member clubs across Canada. Included amongst such member firms are:

The Automobile Association (AA)
The Royal Automobile Club (RAC)
The Royal Scottish Automobile Club
The Royal Irish Automobile Club

Also affiliated are various clubs of the **Alliance Internationale de Tourisme (AIT)**, and **Federation Internationale de l'Automobile (FIA)**.

Membership of affiliated clubs allows access to all services of Canadian associations on production of a membership card.

The motorist is strongly recommended to obtain information available to those intending to drive in Canada, available from **The Automobile Association of Great Britain**. Details are available from local offices or by telephoning: 0256 20123 (AA Head Office).

Police and Accidents

Those involved in road accidents whether directly or indirectly, must remain at the scene until the police arrive to investigate the situation where a serious accident is involved, or else until personal information has passed between all parties and witnesses to a less serious incident. To leave the scene of an accident prematurely, or to refuse to provide assistance one is capable of giving, is viewed as a very serious offence.

One must give personal details (name and address of oneself and owner of the vehicle, along with vehicle registration and other details where appropriate) to police officers or anyone directly involved in the accident.

Money and Banks

In General

Alongside banks, Canadians are serviced by a wide range of trust companies and credit unions. Monetary control is the responsibility of the central institution, the Bank of Canada, which acts as banker to federal and provincial governments as well as commercial banks.

The Currency

The unit of currency, the Canadian dollar, has for several years equated roughly 2 dollars to the British Pound.

The Canadians can no longer boast the strength of their own over their neighbours', the US dollar. In recent times the Canadian dollar has stood at something close to the equivalent of 80 US cents.

Bearing the portrait of Her Majesty Queen Elizabeth II, Canadian notes come in denominations of: $2, $5, $10, $20, $50, $500 and $1,000. A $1 coin was introduced in 1989 to phase out the $1 bill.

US currency is frequently found to be readily acceptable in most heavy tourist areas, particularly those border locations and major towns visited regularly by Americans.

Changing Money

US currency as we have already discussed, is almost universally acceptable throughout Canada. Those entering with foreign currency will find their needs to exchange their cash into the Canadian equivalent well met in all banks and in most post offices.

The wise visitor will take with him or her a reasonable supply of US currency, travellers' cheques, and where possible might convert British currency into Canadian prior to making the journey.

Types of Banks

Chartered banks are the primary institutions, privately owned and operating according to the National Bank Act. Chartered banks operate primarily in the business and commercial sector, recently extending their range of services to long-term loans for business expansion projects, export financing, and so on.

Domestic banks, of which there are 12 in operation, form a national network comprising almost 7,000 branches. The individual is therefore able to obtain the full services of any associated bank in whatever part of Canada he or she might be.

Foreign banks operate throughout Canada, providing expatriates and tourists with the full range of services provided by that same bank in their country of origin.

Trust and Mortgage Companies operate many services similar to those provided in regular banks, as well as operating as largest lender of mortgage capital. Pension fund management, investment and property consultancy services also feature prominently in that range of services covered by this particular institution.

Co-operative credit unions are owned, as the name might suggest, by their members. They usually offer services primarily aimed towards customers in a common industry, trade or community.

Opening a Bank Account

Banking hours are normally 10 am to 3 pm Monday through to Thursday, and 10 am to 5/6 pm on Fridays. Some banks operate extended hours, some opening also on Saturday mornings, but all remain closed on national holidays.

Building societies offer services similar to banks as do their counterparts in Britain. In addition, Canadians have what are known as 'Trust Companies', somewhat similar in structure and operation to building societies, but offering longer opening hours including Saturday services.

Bank accounts can be opened there and then upon presentation of two pieces of personal identification. Usually a local address will be required on one or both pieces of documentation.

Canada Trust, one of the country's leading trust companies, is open six days a week from 9 am to 9 pm. Branches operating throughout the country allow customers instant access to cash without service charges being involved.

Most banking, trust and credit union institutions offer a full range of cheque, saving and other wide-ranging financial services, many accounts providing interest on credit balances.

Banking services are very much similar to those of British banks, including cheque book and cheque card facilities, credit transfer and direct debit services, travellers' cheques and so on. Those entering Canada for all but a short period of time should consider opening an account for themselves in the city or town in which they are located, even if for no other reason than the vast majority of wages and salaries are paid directly into one's bank account.

Importing and Exporting Money

No restrictions are placed on the amount of money visitors may take into Canada.

Cash and Credit Cards

It is almost impossible in Canada, as in many other up-beat parts of the world, to function adequately without at least one cash or credit card to one's name.

Almost all major credit cards are accepted throughout Canada. Most popular are American Express, Visa, Diners and Access. Credit cards, optional in Britain, are more or less essential pre-requisites for everyday life in Canada. For travellers they prove essential, particularly for hotel and car rental payments. In the latter case a large cash deposit might be required if no credit card is available.

Those used to having their cards accepted without question in Britain might be a little over-awed at formalities often encountered over transactions carried out in Canada. Theft and abuse of credit and cash cards has unfortunately for the genuine and credit worthy holder, resulted in a great many often lengthy checks being made on cards presented to retailers, hotels and even banks. One might even be asked for several pieces of supporting personal identification, along with details of address and telephone number. Take it all in the spirit in which it is intended, namely to iron out the rogues in order to protect the interests of those customers credit card companies seek to serve.

The Canadians are a nation of plastic lovers, to a point where many authorities claim that their love of credit cards is now verging on the point of addiction. Recession however, as in most sectors of industry and commerce, has taken its toll on credit card companies, which though still enjoying a high level of membership, have sought to increase plastic spending by means of a wide range of incentives, ranging from varying periods of unlimited medical coverage outside of one's home province, emergency visits from friends and relatives, to up to $200,000 cover against accidental death or dismemberment.

Rates of interest, repayment periods and perks vary between companies, sometimes to a significant degree. The prestige status symbol platinum card for instance, requires an annual fee of around $350, whilst its 'less prestigious' rival green card requires a far lower commitment, currently standing at around $55 per annum.

Traveller's Cheques

The most frequently encountered travellers cheques used throughout Canada are those issued by Thomas Cook, Visa and American Express, all accepted in hotels, restaurants and major stores. In most instances even small-denomination Canadian Dollar travellers cheques will be accepted as cash.

Traveller's cheques provide a safer way of carrying funds than do credit cards and cash. Presented with an authorised signature, traveller's cheques usually present no difficulty in being accepted as cash transactions, and can even be presented for an amount over and above the extent of one's liabilities, with the intention of receiving cash in exchange.

Shopping

Prices

Living costs vary from province to province, and even from one provincial district to the next. The newcomer will not however find their living costs far different to those of British households.

Living standards are high in all parts of Canada.

Taxes

A General Sales Tax (GST) of 7% is currently imposed on all goods and services. Visitors may though reclaim tax on accommodation and any goods which are taken out of the country. GST is not reclaimable on food, drink, tobacco, car hire, transportation and motor homes.

Again, rules and regulations set in individual provinces make for differing levels of provincial sales tax. In Alberta, the Yukon and the Northwest Territories sales tax does not exist; in Newfoundland purchases are inflated to the tune of between 4 and 12%. Such tax is levied on most items purchased in shops, on food in restaurants and other eating establishments, and sometimes on hotel and motel rooms. Provincial sales tax can sometimes be recovered, but only in Nova Scotia, Ontario and Newfoundland.

Various rules and regulations operate by which sales tax may be reduced, fully or partially reclaimed, or eliminated altogether in respect of certain items intended for immediate shipment out of the province.

Remember, as is the case for items subject to Value Added Tax in Britain, prices quoted are not usually inclusive of whatever tax might be levied.

Shopping Hours

The majority of shops are open from 9.30 am to 5.30/6.00 pm. Late evening shopping is available in most major stores, usually on Thursday and Friday evenings, normally extending to 9 pm. In some provinces, depending upon local by-laws, even the smallest of shops are open for extended periods on weekday evenings. Drug and convenience stores usually close at 11 pm. Laws prohibiting Sunday shopping are the subject of ongoing debate, with just as many loyalists at either side of the 'should we/shouldn't we' divide.

Traders, particularly in the more fashionable districts of Toronto, are keen to avail themselves of Sunday opening, much of their arguments based on a growing number of empty retail premises lining their main shopping precinct, all apparently the victims of the recession. Rising rents can not of course be ruled out as a contributory factor to those decisions to quit an already abysmally low level of business activity. That extra day of trading such as a relaxation of the trading laws would allow might well it is argued, prevent a great many more traders from abandoning their premises.

Though early in 1991 laws were passed upholding the abolition of trading on Sundays, a great many traders have seen fit to disobey the authorities. For the time being though, the law-abiding Sunday shopper must rely upon local convenience stores to provide for their needs.

In many densely populated parts, particularly the wealthier locations of Alberta and British Columbia, shopping malls take the obvious financial benefit of extended shopping hours, usually providing for their remaining open until 9.30 pm on week days and from noon until 6 pm on Sunday. For those a little bored with endless hours of shopping – it must be said that very few people seem to suffer such frustrations – many futuristic malls come complete with their own multi-plex cinemas where all the latest films are to be found. In Alberta, the West Edmonton Mall provides over 300 retail outlets, along with an huge skating rink, the 'Fantasyland' indoor amusement park, and an indoor man-made lake complete with wave machine and an assortment of waterslides.

In Vancouver one encounters an amazing assortment of boutiques and handicraft shops, 'amazing' not only because of the hoards of such establishments available, but an adjective that applies equally well to the high quality of goods available. Amongst larger department stores for which this city is particularly popular are Eatons, the Bay and several other nationwide stores. The city, as most other major centres, also has many underground shopping facilities to afford protection to winter spenders.

Toronto is home to the multi-level Eaton Centre, generally regarded as one of the most well-equipped of all North American shopping areas, to the point where many tourists, nationals and non-nationals swear that a day, (you'd actually need longer than that), spent at this centre is like a holiday in its own right.

Shops and Supermarkets

Not surprisingly, given that in many parts of Canada shopping is viewed as more of a hobby than a necessary function of life, shopping malls and precincts abound to such an extent that one might well consider insufficient spending money available to ensure an adequate share to the sheer volume of traders.

Shopping malls proliferate in most popular and wealthier parts of Canada, where one normally finds 50 or more stores all operating under one roof. Restaurants, hamburger bars, cafes, hairdressers, cinemas and hairdressers, complete the complement of facilities available to Canada's growing band of 'professional' shoppers.

Canada's main shopping stores are Eaton's, Woodwards, Simpson's, and the Bay, the latter descended from the pioneering Hudson's Bay Company.

Canadian Food and Food Shopping

A fascinating array of fresh fruits and vegetables is available all year round. From Canada's own domestic resources, her land and the sea surrounding her vast and winding coastline of continent and archipelago, come a wonderful and plentiful supply of bread and grain products, fruit and vegetables, meats and dairy products, and perhaps some of the most delicious and varied of fish and seafood products available in any part of the world.

The wide ethnic origins of Canada's people reflect themselves in the cuisine available in shops, markets (outdoors and inside shopping malls). A visit to Toronto's Kensington and St Lawrence markets will almost certainly leave the visitor with a feeling of having travelled the world in but a few hours, even if one comes away with a feeling that boundless choice and especially high quality of produce, are well matched by the high prices one will be required to pay for the produce one selects.

Non-Food Shopping

A veritable array of fine native handicrafts are available in most parts of the country, including such as wood carvings, pottery, glass, jewellery, knitted and hand-woven goods, moccasins and other articles of Inuit and native clothing.

Shopping by catalogue is a popular pastime in Canada, particularly amongst residents in more remote areas. The growing trend towards shopping by post is the topic of great concern to shop owners, who see their own profits plummeting in line with the increased profits enjoyed by their counterparts in mail order. The reason for such emphasis on shopping by mail? Busy life-styles, two-career families, and the general shortage of certain items in high street stores.

In many ways, shopping for household and non-food consumables very much resembles that with which the British shopper is familiar. One might find one's needs well met in a host of superstores and supermarkets, where the shop's own brands offer a price designed to attract the customer to their products in preference to those of national and multi-national producers' whose items will also be available in great profusion. The shopper will doubtless find a wider variety of products and producers in this country; transportation presents few problems to Canadian shops where goods are shipped from suppliers in all parts of the continent.

For those perhaps a little more discerning in their tastes for non-food consumables and durables, Canada offers a whole host of up market department stores where almost every conceivable product, usually of the highest quality – and price – are available. Despite the fact that most of these stores operate in major towns and cities as one often finds to be the case in Britain, there is usually very little difficulty in having goods delivered to the door, though given that often far greater distances are involved, it might not be that next day delivery we have come to expect in our own little land.

Clothes Shopping

Canadian clothing sizes differ from those of Britain and Europe. Women's clothing for instance ranges from size 5 to 20. Such as jumpers and cardigans normally come in sizes small (S), medium (M), large (L), and extra large (XL).

Not surprisingly, the range of clothing available will largely be determined by the part of Canada in which it is offered for sale. In the colder, sparsely populated areas, very few up-market 'dressy' shops are available – very few people require such garments anyway, since they are unlikely to be seen to good effect under the layers of heavy thick clothing one requires to fight that ongoing battle against the cold. In these outlying areas, a great deal of clothes shopping takes place by post, and even though the market might be proportionately low, catalogue firms tend to fare very nicely indeed from business with their somewhat isolated customers.

The better, classier, designer made clothes are usually available in major towns and cities; Toronto is particularly well served in this respect, as are 'French' centres of Montreal and Quebec city. In Toronto, the most 'fashionable' places to be seen are Yorkville Village and Bloor Street, the city's major fashion centres, where a wide range of Canadian and worldwide designer-labelled attire might be acquired, or given the high price tags accompanying such garments, perhaps 'admired' might be a more appropriate word.

Income Tax

Types of Tax in Canada

Tax is paid on a federal, provincial and municipal basis. Federal rates apply universally though some variations exist in respect of local taxation levels.

Taxable income comprises: employment payments, fees, commissions, dividends, annuities, pension benefits, interest, alimony, maintenance and family allowance payments, unemployment benefits, scholarships, disability benefits, rental and self-employment income.

Levels of Tax

Varying levels of provincial taxation make it difficult to provide any fair indication of what 'off-takes' one might expect from wages. Recent surveys however show that on average, deductions for tax and social security account for very nearly one-third of gross salary.

Dealing with Income Tax

Income tax is deducted in a manner very similar to that of Britain. A PAYE system provides allowances for dependent children, pension contributions, and so on.

All income from whatever source, whether received from within the country or from outside sources, is subject to taxation. A collector assumes responsibility for federal, provincial and territorial taxes in all parts of the country other than Quebec. In Quebec individuals must complete and return an income tax return to the authorities.

For the purposes of deciding domicile, a person who visits Canada for 183 days or more in any year will be deemed for income tax purposes to be a resident of the country.

Tax payers are allocated a Social Insurance Number (SIN), which is subsequently used in all transactions. This number, like the British National Insurance number is used in many various government transactions and is unique to the individual for as long as he or she remains in Canada.

Wage earners and most salaried employees have their income tax deducted at source. Self-employed people and anyone who earns more than 25% of income from other than salaried employment, must pay income tax quarterly.

Law demands that all tax returns are compiled and returned by April 30th each year, with a penalty and interest charge being made on those who submit their documentation after this date.

Those tempted to 'save' a little on their income tax obligations be warned, for the Minister of National Revenue and his able band of investigators have wide-ranging powers, often carried out with the assistance of federal police who are able to enter premises, examine and take copies of books and other documentation, even remove the same from the premises for further investigation.

UK Income Tax

Liability toward the British Inland Revenue authorities is not always entirely absolved the minute one leaves this country for Canada. Much depends upon the time of year (fiscal year) one leaves the country; how much one has earned in this country prior to leaving and how much of the appropriate income tax has been paid; whether one intends to return to Britain during the current tax year; whether one intends to return to Britain at all.

To avoid a heavy tax bill by which to make all that more difficult any future urge you might acquire for repatriation, contact Inland Revenue officials in Britain before you leave for Canada, even if at the time it seems unlikely you will ever return. They will provide you with details of entitlements, obligations, and much useful information relating to your responsibilities in Britain and in your country of intended destination.

Health Insurance

Immediate Requirements

Though at the time of writing there are no official vaccination requirements for entry to Canada, an up-to-date smallpox vaccination may occasionally be required before entry is allowed.

Primary amongst one's considerations before making a move of whatever duration, should be that of medical insurance cover. Canada has nothing equivalent to the National Health Service which we British often take so much for granted.

Canada enjoys a well-deserved reputation as a clean and safe country in which to live. The sheer harshness of Canadian winters however, leads to a higher incidence of road accidents and personal injury than do the winters experienced in Britain. Private insurance is a must; something foreign visitors are able to apply for and obtain immediately upon their arrival by means of registering with the 'Blue Cross'. Emergency accident cover lasts for a maximum 6 months, and must be applied for within 10 days of entering the country.

An alternative and similarly inexpensive insurance scheme is operated via the auspices of:

Hospital Medical Care Plan,
John Ingle Insurance, 710 Bay Street, Toronto.

Those travelling to Canada for whatever intended duration, are advised to take out medical insurance in their own country.

Obtaining Health Insurance

As soon as an individual becomes a legal permanent resident in Canada, he or she becomes entitled to health insurance benefits, and should therefore register with local health authorities immediately such permanent status is confirmed.

Insurance schemes provided by the Canadian government are fully comprehensive but still consumes an often hefty chunk of one's income for premiums involved.

A state sponsored national health insurance scheme provides for ten interrelated provincial hospital and healthcare programmes, funded through taxation or premium charges in conjunction with federal authorities.

Canada's national health insurance programme provides for all permanent residents of the country, and under this scheme citizens are not required to make any contribution towards certain medical and hospital expenses.

The Canada Health Act with which all provinces must apply in formulating their own health care plans, provides for cover in respect of essential hospital services, dental surgery carried out in hospital, doctor's fees, and in some instances cover is provided for such as drugs and dental care.

There is no universal dental insurance scheme in operation, though several private schemes are available.

Provincial government has full responsibility for health and the operation of two insurance programmes – one for hospital treatment, the other for alternative forms of medical care. Many private insurance schemes operate throughout Canada, usually with appropriate deductions from wages and salaries.

Total health care expenditure in 1988 was an estimated 8.7% of GNP.

Hospitals and Medical Treatment

Hospitals

Hospitals in Canada are of the very highest standard, as are the medical charges one will be expected to pay for treatment.

At the time of writing charges for adult inpatients range from $250 – $600 a day; charges for children in specialized hospitals range from $200 to $800 per day. What might seem a very large sum indeed compared to Britain's system of health care, is in some provinces subject to an additional 30% surcharge imposed on non-resident patients.

Social Security

The Department of National Health and Welfare administers all health and welfare programmes, with four branches bearing specific responsibility for its own special sector:

The Health Protection Branch is responsible for supervision and control of drugs and medical equipment and devices.

The Health Services and Promotions Branch is charged with responsibility for promoting and publicising the means and ease of access to appropriate health care.

The Fitness and Amateur Sports Branch co-ordinates and develops sport and personal fitness programmes on a national and international level.

The Medical Services Branch oversees the needs of ethnic groups, primarily immigrant and indigenous Indian populations.

The Benefits

Family allowance is paid in respect of all dependent children under the age of 18, on condition that at least one parent is a permanent resident or citizen of Canada and has paid income tax for at least one year.

The standard age for retirement is 65; all persons of this age and over who meet residency requirements will receive Old Age Security (OAS), a monthly retirement pension sometimes supplemented where other income is limited. CPP, the Canada Pension Plan, is another form of income protection, designed to supplement other pensions and sources of income, as well as provide insurance in case of death or disability. Earnings and contributions determine the amount beneficiaries might ultimately expect to receive from the plan, and contributions are compulsory for almost all workers, employers and self-employed persons, other than in the province of Quebec, where a similar plan, the QPP (Quebec Pension Plan), makes roughly similar provisions.

Low income families are eligible for Guaranteed Income Supplement (GIS), a monthly amount which is based on the previous year's income. Families are means-tested before eligible for such payments.

Various forms of unemployment and disability benefits are paid to those in need, and an extensive range of refresher and retraining facilities are provided throughout. In November 1990, Canada's Unemployment Insurance Act provided for wide ranging and generous improvements to the benefits paid in unemployment, maternity, sickness and family allowances. Though retirement age is officially 65, workers may continue if they wish usually to the age of 70; the Act also extended unemployment insurance to those workers past normal retirement age.

Your National Insurance Records

Whether entering the country for the purpose of employment lasting but a few weeks or intending instead to spend the rest of your working life there, you will need to take with you some details relating to your British national insurance records, most importantly your National Insurance number. If you aren't already in possession of usual documentation carrying your NI number (medical card, national insurance card, income tax documentation and so on), then contact your local Department of Social Security where you will be provided with at least some official indication of your status within the British Social Security system.

Canada – The Social Scene

In General

Opportunities for a wide and varied range of leisure pursuits present themselves in all parts of Canada; in major towns and cities one might enjoy that exciting nightlife – discos, bars and restaurants to which they have become accustomed to from living in Britain. But a short distance away from many such centres of activity there will usually be ample scope to enjoy the great – and we mean 'great' outdoors – whether for the purposes of taking part in countless leisure and sporting facilities or simply to admire and enjoy some of the world's most breathtaking scenery. There are facilities in almost all towns and cities for a wide range of indoor sporting pursuits. Those with less active ambitions in Canada might enjoy some of most exciting of shopping malls, and take in a film or two in the cinema provided for those seeking a little break from the Canadian national interest of shopping.

But, even with so glowing a social life awaiting the newcomer to this magnificent country, it must be remembered that many parts are entirely devoid of anything by which to fill one's out of work hours – totally devoid not only of sporting, shopping, and leisure facilities, but totally lacking too in that usually most important of leisure-interest accoutrements – people!

The message here is simple – exactly which part of Canada you decide to make your home will entirely determine those leisure interest and social facilities at your disposal, as will population density for which those facilities seek to cater. The beachcomber will not therefore find his or her heaven in the frozen wastes of northern regions; the potential recluse will though find Utopia in that wild uninhabited land mass, though doubtless little or anything in the way of employment by which to cater for his or her maintenance. Ah well, we can't have everything, can we?

Due to the sheer size of this country and the diversity of population density and ethnic groups within, individuals deciding to live in Canada, whether temporarily or permanently, will find much useful information available to them regarding amongst other things, those leisure facilities available in the area of their choice, simply by contacting local tourist information offices. Details of local offices are provided in that earlier section 'City by City, Region by Region', to which the readers' attention is drawn. Canadian tourist information officers incidentally, are renowned the world over for their helpful assistance to nationals, migrants and foreigners alike.

Canadian Society

Given that around 80 per cent of Canadians live close to their country's border with the United States, habits, customs and life styles are understandably similar to those of their neighbours. Many Canadians would not however thank you for voicing such an opinion, given as they are to an overwhelmingly strong sense of national identity. Many see themselves as far less brash, and infinitely more genteel than their cousins in more southerly regions of their shared continent.

Strong cultural ties with Europe, in some parts very close ties with France, make for a way of life that for many takes on a far more European than American flavour.

Tips

Tips and service charges are not usually included in bills. As in neighbouring USA, a tip of 10 – 15% is the norm in most Canadian restaurants. Tips are usually offered to hairdressers and barbers, taxi drivers, bellhops, doormen, redcaps (porters), particularly where service has proved exemplary. Porters at airports and railway stations are normally rewarded with $1 per item of luggage carried.

Out of Hours Relaxation

Perhaps it comes as no surprise to realise that most Canadians spend the majority of their leisure hours out of doors, enjoying the magnificent scenery and boundless leisure pursuits their country has to offer.

Canada's harsh winters explain a distinct preference for family relaxation in front of the television set. Television stations abound, with programmes broadcast in major languages French and English, and some in a wide variety of minority languages. Many television programmes are also imported from neighbouring United States, and video entertainment too adds to the luxury of that little spot from which to hide from the cold outdoors.

City dwellers though do not always find their out of hours relaxation hampered by the weather, for to the rescue comes the Canadian planner and a host of blueprints for underground leisure facilities, shopping precincts, cinemas, sports centres and so on.

And of course it is proximity to major centres which will ultimately determine the range of leisure facilities available to the population by which to enjoy their out of working hours. For many, outdoor sports available even in and around major cities are the real attraction of life in Canada.

And from wide ethnic origins such as lie at the heart of Canada's population, comes a superb array of drinking and eating establishments: foreign restaurants take the diner to almost any part of the world he or she might care to visit; pubs can even bring the homesick 'Briton' back to good old Blighty, even if just for a few hours spent in one or two of the many typically English pubs springing up in most major towns and cities.

If it hasn't occurred to the reader already, to the Canadians' great credit, it must be said that nationals and immigrants alike take their leisure hours very seriously indeed, and commerce along with government authorities see to it that everything the leisure seeker needs is well and truly catered for.

Drinking

'Heavy' drinkers be careful, for 'heavy' is not a word used so much to indicate quantity of consumption as the high level of alcohol one normally finds in Canadian beers; far higher a level than that of their neighbouring American brewers. Thankfully – perhaps not though when the after effects reveal themselves – it is also allegedly a great deal more palatable than that from across the border. English and Australian beers also prove very popular in Canada, and almost all ales and beers from whatever country their recipe emanates, come in lagers, pilsners, ales and becks.

The main Canadian brewing companies, Molson-Carling and Labatt, tend to dominate the range of beers and lagers available throughout the country, sharing between them around 90% of Canada's lager industry. Each has its own unique and highly original brew: Carling's Buckeye, Labatt's IPA and Molson's Braider. A number of smaller regional breweries such as Moosehead and Creemore Springs are now making their presence known to the big boys in the brewing trade.

And those of us who envisage wine growing regions as subject to eternal summer-time climatic conditions, might be more than a little surprised to discover that many parts of a country which receives far more than its fair share of snow, are also renowned for producing numerous exquisite wines.

Since individual provinces are responsible for their own drinking –
or liquor laws – rules and regulations regarding legal opening times
and drinking age vary from one part of Canada to the next. In some
provinces rigid and strict laws relate to the selling of alcohol, with
only a very few retail outlets being licensed by the authorities.

As an example of the regional differences one encounters in
drinking laws, the minimum age for drinking in Alberta, Manitoba,
Quebec and Prince Edward Island is 18 years; everywhere else you
must wait another year for the honour of legally purchasing and
consuming alcoholic beverages.

Opening hours of bars and other times during which alcohol may
be sold or consumed, owe as much to the origins of the early settlers
of individual provinces as to those laws laid down by their
descendants.

Government-operated 'off-licences' generally maintain normal
shopping hours, that is 9 am to 5.30 pm. Beer and liquor stores all
close on national holidays.

Despite the image many might hold of the average American as
permanent 'can-toter', the Canadians actually consume more alcohol
than either the Americans or the British, though usually much of it is
consumed indoors as an accompaniment to whichever of a wealth of
television programmes one decides to view. Whether this form of
social drinking is by reason of choice or for the fact that drinking in
public places, other than specially licensed drinking places is strictly
illegal, is a matter for conjecture. Suffice to say that anyone found
drinking alcohol in public places, such as beaches and sports
grounds, will run the risk of having their drinks confiscated by the
police and the contents immediately emptied down the nearest
drain.

Canadian bars tend to fall between those best termed 'dives' and
the up-market variety we in Britain might instead call 'wine bars'.
Very few middle of the range establishments such as those most
frequently found in Britain are to be found in Canada.

Eating

Not surprisingly, given the wide diversity of ethnic origins of
today's Canadian citizens, dining out can take one to almost any
corner of the world – palate-wise that is – for here restaurants abound
offering the delicacies of Canada's multinational background:
Ukrainian, Japanese, French, German, Italian, Vietnamese,
Hungarian and Middle Eastern dishes are readily available in almost
all major centres. Toronto in particular is noted for its wide range of
foreign cuisine.

Additionally, each province and usually different regions within provinces, are noted for their own dishes and unique styles of cooking. In Newfoundland one must not for instance miss out on sampling cod dish 'Brewis', flipper pie or even fried cod's tongues; in Quebec it is 'habitant' cooking and French cuisine that will invariably feature as order of the day. Some of Quebec's most popular menus date back to 1646, to a time when the Ursuline sisters of Quebec adapted their traditional Norman cooking to local ingredients. British Columbia boasts salmon and king crab, whilst the northern territories are renowned for delicious Arctic grayling and char. In Manitoba a particular delicacy is Winnipeg Goldeye – fish smoked over oak logs and then dyed a deep coral.

In actual fact there are very few dishes one could describe as uniquely Canadian, although many would argue that what bear and groundhog dishes one can sometimes locate would more than adequately fit the description. Perhaps though that most closely approximating 'unique' Canadian dish is families' favourite pancakes, liberally covered with maple syrup.

Apart from the excellent fish and certain meat dishes one often discovers peculiar to certain parts of the country, eating out in Canada can actually prove an almost identical experience to that of the average outdoors cuisine enjoyed in the United States: hamburger joints, fast food outlets, steak bars, and a vast array of 'delivered-straight-to-your-door' services are available in almost every populous centre to which one might venture.

Theatre/Cinema etc.

Cinemas and theatre lovers need not worry that winter will find them instead seated in front of the television screen, for here cinemas and theatres operate above and below ground level.

Facilities are available almost everywhere for the enjoyment of French and English films and plays. In Vancouver there is an especially strong theatre following, with many superb facilities available for their entertainment in the downtown cinemas of Granville Mall.

Toronto offers excellent music, theatre, ballet and operatic productions at the O'Keefe Centre. The city in fact has its own symphony orchestra resident in the Roy Thomson Hall.

For film lovers, Toronto is a hard venue to beat. In September the Toronto Film Festival screens some of the most recent films, many of them enjoying their premiere in a wide variety of cinemas ranging from downtown movie theatres to a sumptuous six storey high cinesphere.

Culture/History

Music, architecture, museums and art galleries, all are adequately catered for in all major towns and cities.

Vancouver is particularly rich in fine art galleries, and is noted too for the excellent facilities offered to lovers of music and the opera.

Toronto's Art Gallery houses some of the world's finest collections, amongst them many exquisite sculptures, and a wide variety of international works of art.

Nightlife

Gamblers will find their activities seriously curtailed in all parts of this massive country, where gambling in casinos is illegal except for one small exception, namely in the gold rush town of Dawson City in the Yukon, where gambling is permitted at a reconstruction of Diamond Tooth Gertie's casino.

Amongst those seeking to gamble without making tracks towards Diamond Gertie's, lotteries prove extremely popular; tickets are available at almost all stationery shops and newsagents. So popular in fact has the dream ticket become, that critics suggest government finances grow steadily richer, whilst the punter grows ever poorer at the expensive of that impossible dream, now bringing in proportionately more income from taxation than any other commodity with the exception of tobacco.

It is perhaps to Toronto that the real night-owl should direct his or her attentions, for here the sheer number and variety of clubs available is enough to provide a lifetime of revelling with never a day of boredom to spoil the prospect.

Bars and clubs tend on the whole to attract a certain specific clientele, many of them catering to young professionals making their way to the top, others seeking instead to serve the interests of less ambitious individuals more intent on clambering their way to the top of the social ladder.

And whilst The Yonge and St. Clair areas cater more for the young set, in Downtown Toronto one discovers a wealth of stylish hotel lounges designed instead to attract the custom of 'youngish' customers – we'd perhaps refer to them in Britain as 'middle aged and over'! Close to the University of Toronto, one might be forgiven for thinking that Britain had suddenly re-appeared for no apparent reason, for here the growing trend is towards typical English pubs – whether 'pie and mash' is on the menu yet is something you will have to find out for yourself!

Toronto aside however, in almost all cities and major centres one will discover a nightlife comparable with that of almost any other part of the world. Hard-working Canadians are not deprived of activities by which to fill their leisure time, even though a great many would far prefer a seat in front of the television set with a can of beer or lager ready to hand.

Sports

The most popular outdoor activities we find are usually the side-products of those long harsh winters for which Canada is renowned: skiing, ice skating and ice hockey, snow-shoeing and ice-fishing.

Swimming, tennis and golf are also amongst the most popular sporting activities, for which enjoyment facilities in all provinces are of an excellent standard. Curling, basketball, volleyball, rugby, windsurfing, sky diving, horse riding and rodeo riding all feature prominently amongst a host of other indoor and outdoor sporting and recreational activities.

A wealth of lakes, coastline and magnificent open spaces consequently make hunting and fishing popular outdoor pursuits. Regulations, licensing and hunting seasons very from one province to the next. Hunting is not permitted at any time in national parks. Fishing is usually permitted in national parks, where one must obtain a necessary permit from park officials.

In those places in which hunting and fishing are permitted, all non-residents must purchase provincial hunting and fishing permits, available from most post offices.

Mention spectator sports, and it is to the local hockey rink you will find the majority of Canadians flocking. As soon as children can skate they learn to play what, if the number of organised leagues is anything to go by, must surely deserve pride of place as first national winter sport.

All provinces have not only their own hockey team, but baseball too features high on the calendar of spectator sports for most Canadians; though relatively new to the sport, many provincial league teams now play to world class status.

The Great Outdoors

And perhaps nowhere on earth is the great outdoors as 'great' as that one discovers in Canada, whether in terms of gross size or sheer unadulterated beauty.

Most provinces have dedicated vast stretches of land to parks and open spaces, for enjoyment in their own right or for the many camping and hiking facilities they contain, usually alongside a host of other opportunities to enjoy oneself canoeing, fishing, observing nature and photographing wildlife and scenery.

All provinces and territories have at least one national park; in all there are 29 almost all reliably and efficiently serviced by the Trans-Canada Highway. Rigidly enforced rules govern those entering national parks, who must not attempt to feed bears; must place their litter only in specially provided containers; must inform the park warden or staff before going into the further reaches of the park, and who must also comply with one of the most tightly enforced laws of all, namely that hunting is under no circumstances permitted in national parks.

Details regarding National Parks is available from:

Parks Canada,
Ottawa, Ontario, K1A 1G2. Tel: 819 997 2800

Wildlife Watching

Roaming bison, whales circling the Pacific shores, Rocky mountain goats climbing high in craggy terrain – wondrous indeed for the eye to perceive – but a bear set on attacking its transfixed spectator might present not quite so exhilarating an experience! Consequently, before roaming free in national parks, visitors are required to register their presence with park officials, who will advise on safe and dangerous locations, as well as procedures to follow should one nevertheless encounter potentially life-threatening situations.

Various little-known techniques are available to the adventurous tourist, aimed towards warding off bears and other potentially dangerous animals. Such devices include bear-scarers, a type of bell worn around the neck, by which to warn the animal of your presence in the locality. Such warning incidentally is one not designed to lessen the distance between you and a hungry animal, as much as to allow the bear to take steps to protect its young against intruders, one of the primary causes of attacks against humans. A further common cause of attack is that of being suddenly scared by intruders, the latter of course adding credence to the wearing of that bell around one's neck, and park officials' frequent warnings to make as much – but not sudden – noise as possible in outlying areas, so as not to catch wildlife by surprise. Let them know you're there and they will doubtless leave you alone, whilst maintaining a safe distance for themselves and their young.

Children and Schools

Education is free for all up to final secondary school level; starting age is between 6 and 7, and leaving is allowed between the ages of 15 or 16 depending upon specific regulations laid down by individual authorities.

Each province bears full responsibility for the organisation and administration of educational facilities within its boundaries. Education falls universally into four broad levels: pre-school, elementary, secondary and post-secondary. Recent surveys reveal that Alberta invests more heavily per capita in education and career development than does any other province.

Educational policies differ between provinces, all of which are legally obliged to recognize certain minority language and denominational rights.

French-speaking children are entitled by law to receive all lessons in French. In Quebec, the children of all immigrants are registered in French schools. In this province, a recent task force has called for changes thereby allowing the children of some migrants to study in English, something they feel would not unduly threaten 'francophone Quebeckers'.

A dual system of public/private school operates along lines similar to that which operates in Britain. More and more parents are opting for private education, particularly in the provinces of British Columbia and Quebec, where a heavy emphasis on academic subjects finds favour with a large proportion of more wealthy immigrant families. In Canada most private schools are Roman Catholic. The public school system is free whilst children are within compulsory ages for attendance. At pre-school level, fees are frequently charged.

Higher education is provided in around 70 universities and some 200 colleges. Student loans and other forms of financial aid are available to offset or cover the cost of annual fees. Federal loans usually available, are repayable over a period of up to ten years. Recent studies of international educational systems reveal that in the main Canada's higher secondary level students tend to perform significantly better than most of their counterparts in other countries.

Education for those in the 10 – 14 year old bracket also proved markedly superior to that of most other civilized countries of the world. Standards reached their peak in British Columbia and Ontario. There is though a dull side to this coin, with results seemingly only applied to non-scientific subjects; Canadian children do not allegedly outdo their peers in such as biology, chemistry and physics.

A recent article in 'Canada News', states that the province of Alberta is home to a higher percentage of degree-qualified employees than any other Canadian province, and nearly 40% of the population possesses some form of post-secondary education. Figures are highest in Calgary and Edmonton, where around 1 in every 5 adults possesses a degree, diploma or secondary education certificate.

Useful Information

Amongst the most renowned of private educational establishments are the following:

St. George's School for Boys,
Vancouver, British Columbia.

Shawnigan Lake School,
(a boarding school for boys and girls aged between 8 and 12 years),
Vancouver Island, British Columbia.

Schools – General Points

All provinces have full responsibility for education within their boundaries, and consequently standards and curriculum can vary often dramatically between provinces.

In all parts, education is divided into four levels: pre-school, elementary, secondary and post-secondary education.

Registration procedures vary between provinces; the best advice that can therefore be given to parents intending to take their children to Canada for any length of time is, once that vital decision as to where to live has been made, contact the local Board of Education for the province concerned, to discuss the matter concerning suitable educational facilities. 'School Boards' are listed in all telephone directories.

The school year extends to something in the region of 200 days, usually beginning in early September and closing towards the end of June. A few provinces however, operate certain full-time private educational establishments, catering primarily for international pupils and students.

Schools operate from Monday to Friday, as is usually the case in Britain, but unlike that educational system with which most British school children are familiar, the learning day normally begins at 8.30 am and finishes between 3.00 and 3.30 pm.

When registering a child in a Canadian school, parents should where possible, take whatever school records are available from their education in Britain. Many schools actually insist on original documentation incidentally, and will not accept photocopies. Once that decision to leave for Canada has been made, parents should therefore approach British education authorities for such documentation, making for a far easier process of acquisition than might be experienced if making the very same request from a distance of thousands of miles away. This is not to say however, that those children who come minus their personal documentation will be placed at any distinct disadvantage. Usually children in such instances will be graded temporarily until their educational abilities can be accurately assessed for more realistic methods of grading.

Roman Catholics desiring their children's attendance at a Roman Catholic school should contact the Separate School Board for further information of the options open to them. Local telephone directories provide appropriate addresses under 'Board of Education' or 'Separate School Board', or else the name of the school of your choice if known.

Useful Addresses

Youth and Student Information, Association of Student Councils,
171 College Street, Toronto, Ontario, Canada, M5T 1PZ.

Canadian Bureau for International Education,
85 Albert Street, 14th Floor, Ottawa, Ontario, Canada, K1P 6A4.

Children in Canada

For many parents making the move to Canada, it is the future of their children that presents the greatest potential problem, often culminating in a decision to abandon the prospect of emigrating. In truth however, there are very few insurmountable problems that are likely to present themselves where the lives and well-being of one's children are concerned.

In moving to Canada, the most common concern to many parents is the influence of the French language upon their children. Will they find the language difficult to learn? Will they find themselves at a marked disadvantage until such time as they acquire at least a working knowledge of French? How much of the language do they need to learn in the first place? Will they be required to attend a primarily French-speaking school? Is there any method by which parents can assist their children in acquiring some knowledge of the language either before they leave for Canada, or else during their first few months in their new homeland?

Potential problems of adjusting to life in a new country, discovering new friends, learning new ways and customs, perhaps even acquiring a taste for as yet untested foods and regional dishes – all cause unnecessary and wasted hours of worry to parents. Children actually take very little time to adjust to new surroundings; far less time and trouble than we adults credit them with. And often, the younger the child the better able he or she is to acclimatise to whatever changes in environment. Remember too, that in most parts of Canada there are heavy British expatriate communities, and many clubs and organisations to which the newcomer might turn for help and advice during those early days in their new country.

Yet still there are parents whose prime interest is that of retaining the essential British personality of their children, particularly those whose stay in Canada is not expected to be one of any real length of time. For these parents the preference might be for children to attend boarding schools in Britain whilst their parents attend to whatever reason their visit to Canada entails. In some instances, one parent remains in Britain with the children; at other times grandparents or relatives in Britain are assigned responsibility for children until their parents' return.

Education – The Options

There are several options open to parents considering the best potential for their children's education. Amongst them are:

Boarding Schools in the United Kingdom

For obvious purposes, an option more appropriate to those living and working in Canada for but a limited period of time, at least parents will find some solace in the fact that their children will remain in that British way of life to which they most likely are accustomed. The effect on the child must of course assume paramount importance; those children already used to boarding school education will hardly be likely to notice the effect of their parents venturing abroad for a short while; those used to being with their parents day in and day out might instead find their lives made little short of miserable when suddenly placed in new surroundings with no back up support such as their tightly knit family life might hitherto have provided.

Those contemplating this option for their children might find 'The Parents Guide to Independent Schools' very useful indeed. This booklet is available from:

SFIA Educational Trust,
FIA House, 15 Forlease Road, Maidenhead, Berks, SL6 1JA.
0628 34291

Further information on boarding schools in the United Kingdom is available from:

Independent Schools Information Service (ISIS),
56 Buckingham Gate, London, SW1E 2AH. 071 630 8793

State Schools in Canada

A very realistic option for those contemplating more than a brief visit to Canada, where educational facilities are renowned for their high standard, and great care is taken to integrate children from whatever national origins into the day-to-day educational system.

For further information concerning international and domestic educational establishments contact the following:

Canadian Bureau for International Education,
85 Albert Street, 14th Floor, Ottawa, Ontario, Canada, K1P 6A4.

Correspondence Courses

An option perhaps best suited to those whose children might be already studying for British qualifications for which examinations will be taken upon their intended return to Britain.

Many such courses are available for children from pre-school age to 18 years of age and over. One college providing a full range of courses for children and adults is:

Mercers College,
Ware, Hertfordshire, SG12 8BU. 0920 465926

For full details of schools available contact:

Council for the Accreditation of Correspondence Colleges,
27 Marylebone Road, London, NW1 5JS. 071 935 5391

Home Teaching

Highly appropriate where short-term visits to other countries are involved, this is an option that comes with professional advice and back up support by which to allow parents, even those without any academic or teaching qualifications, to personally teach their children. Full details are available from:

Worldwide Educational Service School System (WES),
10 Barley Mow Passage, Chiswick, London, W4 4PH. 081 994
   3622

Useful Information

Details of international schools are available from:

European Council of International Schools (ECIS),
18 Lavant Street, Petersfield, Hants, GU32 3EW. 0730 68244

Retirement in Canada

The Possibilities

Recent surveys conducted by the British Department of Trade and Industry, suggest that around 11% of Canada's population is over 65 years of age, a rate though currently lower than that of most European countries, is in fact growing at around three times faster than the population itself. The largest proportion of retired citizens live in the Atlantic provinces and in British Columbia.

Canada divides its retired citizens into the 'young-old', namely those aged between standard retirement age 65 and 75, and the acknowledged 'old', being those whose years extend beyond that youthful 75.

A survey completed in the early 1990s placed Canada as a retirement destination only second to Australia in terms of the number of pensioners who have retired here from other parts of the world. The Department of Social Security estimates that around 100,000 British pensioners have made Canada their retirement home. Many it seems set out to join children who have already migrated, envisaging it seems an ideal family reunion in a country where living standards, opportunities and life style in general are much improved upon what their homeland has to offer.

All too often though, the dream quickly becomes a nightmare, when it is realised that advancing years offer little protection against harsh Canadian winters; resultant high medical expenses are often the deciding factor in seeking that passage 'home'.

Yet still today's elderly Canadians enjoy a far more affluent and healthier standard of living that their counterparts of years gone by; a standard which also far and away exceeds that of many other countries of the world. Amongst the 'young-old' there exists a high proportion of married couple households.

Is Retirement to Canada a Feasible Proposition?

Even if young and healthy when making that initial move to Canada, it is wise to consider whether one might ultimately elect to live out one's retirement years in that country, or else return to Britain. In reality, those who have opted for migration to Canada rarely return to Britain, unless their children have decided to make that earlier 'repatriation' to their parents' former homeland.

As a clean, healthy and safe place to live, Canada has much to offer its retired citizens. Leisure facilities also provide much to fill one's new-found freedom.

Rules and regulations relating to retirement for those not born in Canada are in fact very relaxed and easy to understand.

What Permits are Needed?

That person granted status as a landed immigrant, will be treated in all ways on retirement as will Canadian nationals. Those in their middle years, perhaps unsure of what benefits might be transferable from British pensions and from benefits accrued whilst working in Canada, should contact British Social Security Offices, the main branch of which is detailed later, as well as seek appropriate information from Canadian government officials based in Britain.

Officially, a person applying to retire to Canada, is one who has reached the age of 55 and does not intend to take up employment once inside the country. That person's application will be reviewed by immigration authorities, taking several prime considerations into account. Those factors that will go to making for acceptance or otherwise include the following:

- The area of intended destination
- Whether friends and relatives already reside in that locality
- The applicant's potential for adjusting to life in his or her new country
- Whether or not the applicant has sufficient financial resources to support him or herself and dependants without need to resort to State aid of municipal, provincial or federal variety

Generally, those persons who can adequately satisfy immigration officials of their suitability, taking into account all of these factors, should find little problem in obtaining a fairly straightforward and speedy authorisation for retirement to Canada.

Where to Live

Those retiring to Canada to join relatives, usually opt to live with those relatives until suitable accommodation for themselves is found. Alternatively, many elect to rent their homes on a month-to-month or other short-term arrangement whilst carrying out their job hunting expedition.

That part of Canada in which to live is one that can take a great many factors into account, almost certainly paramount amongst them being whether or not the retired person or couple have relatives or friends already living in the country. For many that decision to retire to Canada is motivated by a desire for proximity to their children who might have made the transition many years before.

Certainly in one's later years, Canada's harsh climate must be taken into account. Regular mention is made in 'Canada News' of the impact that harsh winter climate has on the less youthful of newcomers to the country, often culminating in illness, depression, and consequently proving a burden on one's health insurance premiums. There is it seems, a high repatriation rate amongst those who retire to Canada, who are less than fully aware of just how powerful an adversary a Canadian winter can be.

House and Home

Condominiums are proving increasingly popular with retired citizens. Usually such accommodation comprises an apartment or a row (terraced) house, one which is usually purchased but requires an additional rental charge to cover maintenance of outside areas, snow clearance, refuse collection and so on.

As is often the case for retired persons living in Britain, once one's family has left home that large house might be viewed as cumbersome and occupying far too much of one's new found leisure time to keep it clean and tidy. Consequently, many newly or soon to retire individuals and couples find themselves seeking out smaller premises in which to spend their retirement.

The actual province in which to live is entirely for the individual to determine, usually that decision taking quite obvious personal factors and preferences into account: whether one has children, friends and relatives living in Canada and where; whether one prefers the leisure facilities offered by one region over another; whether one is content to remain in that province in which he or she has lived and worked for perhaps many years before.

Money and Pensions

More affluent than their peers in many other parts of the world, and indeed their Canadian counterparts of past generations, the retired of Canada's population enjoy a relatively high income from both public and private pensions. In addition over three-quarters of retired citizens live in fully-paid for homes, have no dependent children to support, and have access to most medical and recreational services provided at little or no cost to themselves.

Pensions can be any or a combination of three types: state, company and private. Agreements and reciprocal arrangements exist between Britain and many other countries of the world including Canada, providing for the transfer of British pensions to Britons intending to retire abroad. British pensions are frozen at that level existing at the time of transfer, meaning of course that no account will be taken of pension increases in line with retail and price inflation.

All British Social Security offices can provide details to help with the transition from Britain to Canada, by means of personal advice and printed documentation available in leaflet BR19. Specific information from experienced officers is available from:

The Department of Health and Social Security (Overseas Group), Benton Park Road, Newcastle-upon-Tyne, NE98 1YX. 091 225 3002

A Canadian state pension comprises a basic sum supplemented by an earnings-related amount. Qualification for all or part of the basic state pension requires payment of National Insurance contributions for a period of at least six years.

Depending upon personal circumstances and whether the individual actually takes up employment in Canada, he or she might in addition to British and Canadian state pensions, be entitled to private pensions from employers and private pension funds in both countries. A seemingly complicated matter might present itself in an entitlement to two state pensions, two company pensions, and two private pensions. Most pensions schemes are however well administered, and in general there should be no difficulty in having British pensions transferred to Canada. Nor should one worry that a watchful eye is essential if entitlement is to be accurately assessed and promptly received. If in doubt, British and Canadian Social Security officers will be more than happy to assist, as will accountants and financial advisors in either country.

Income Tax

To eliminate any potential difficulties existing in relation to income tax responsibilities for those intending to retire to Canada, one should seek advice and information from British Inland Revenue offices and whatever expatriate groups he or she belongs to.

The immigrant should obtain a declaration from the new country's taxation authorities, to the effect that he or she is, or will be resident in the new country for tax purposes and will be taxed there for income received from whatever part of the world. This documentation must be presented as soon as possible to Inspectors of the British Inland Revenue, if one is to eliminate the possibility of automatically facing a deduction of a 25% withholding tax. Such deduction however painful it might at first be, does not usually take the form of an irretrievable 'fine', and usually is repaid when one's tax status in the new country is determined.

Health and Hospitals

That section relating to health, hospitals and medical facilities applies equally to retired people in Canada, who will find standards at least as good as those we enjoy in Britain, and waiting lists perhaps a good deal shorter.

Private health care plans are a good idea in almost every country of the world, and particularly so in Canada where state healthcare facilities do not exist on a scale anywhere near that of the British National Health Service.

That private insurance might of course be taken out during one's entry to Canada many decades before; it might instead be initiated at the end of one's working life in Britain which is intended to be followed by retirement in Canada. Many factors, primary amongst them age, will determine that premium one might be required to make for appropriate health care insurance, and should be considered fully prior to entry to Canada in the case of retired immigrant applicants.

To reiterate, the one great problem to present itself to those entering or already enjoying their retirement years, is the harshness of the Canadian winter, a sad fact that can lead to many related illnesses amongst young and more so amongst the 'young old' and elderly.

Wills and Death

We are of course making grand plans for life once that decision to live and work in Canada for whatever duration has finally been taken, yet sadly the fact of death must also be taken into account and steps taken to ensure that one's final wishes will be adequately and accurately carried out; that estate, responsibilities and liabilities will be taken care of by whoever one chooses to assign the task.

If you die intestate, that is without making a valid will, then your estate will be administered according to Canadian law. Though similar in many ways to British law, you can if you wish, have your will made in a manner more approaching the British law on wills and administration of deceased persons' estates. Consult your solicitor in whatever country, for a full analysis of what differences might exist between Canadian and British laws relating to wills and administration of estates.

Exactly which country one selects as final resting place is of course a matter for personal preference, suffice to say that procedures and fees for the return of a body to Britain for burial or cremation will doubtless be long and costly. Canadian funerals can however prove costly in themselves, and as often happens now in Britain, many individuals and couples take out funeral insurance policies whereby to relieve their dependants of high costs by which to add to their already low emotional state.

Those for whom Canada has been home for perhaps several decades, usually decide to make that country the one in which their remains will be 'disposed' of, often because their closest relatives share their homeland. Those who instead choose to be returned to Britain should discuss the matter with lawyers and consulate officials, or if death occurs without having taken such advice, have their dependants or legal advisors consult British government officials in Canada for details, rules and regulations concerning repatriation.

Daily Life

That person already used to life in Canada when retirement finally comes, will of course already be aware of what facilities exist for the fulfilment of their retirement plans. 'Retirement shock' though is a very real possibility, as indeed is the case in whatever part of the world one lives. That sudden break with the habits of often many decades; the rising at a certain hour; the companionship of working colleagues; the actual tasks and responsibilities of work itself – all once removed from daily life can prove all too much of a strain on those who have not planned adequately for their retirement.

Most Canadian employers in common with their British counterparts, provide retirement training courses for those employees approaching the appropriate age for leaving the workforce. Such training might often seem wholly inappropriate and unnecessary to that person shortly to retire, but in fact should never be taken lightly, for much scientific, medical and social evidence suggests that an employee who is aware of what to expect from retirement, who is 'taught' how best to use those extra hours, advised on management of a potentially reduced income, will find that transition from worker to retiree far smoother and infinitely less painful than will the person for whom retirement 'training' is viewed as pointless.

Those intending to retire to Canada once their working days in Britain have ended, should take whatever opportunity presents itself to learn as much as possible about their intended new homeland. If amongst that list of learning possibilities one can include a visit, then so much the better. Given that many newly retired entrants to Canada have made their move to join relatives for whom this is already home, there is every chance that such individuals and couples have already visited the country perhaps on several occasions previously.

Certainly the retired will find much to occupy their daily lives. Canadian pensions are usually sufficient to provide for over and above the everyday essentials of life: accommodation, food, clothing and such, and most retired people find sufficient finances left over to enjoy a relatively active social life. Whatever form that social life takes is as for many things a matter of personal preference, although Canadian society is renowned for catering adequately for the needs of its less than youthful citizens.

Walking, cycling, touring, sight-seeing, eating out, drinking, even participating in many of the cold-weather sports for which Canada is famed the world over, all feature high on the agenda for retired persons.

Those perhaps a little less active, whether an enforced or conscious decision, will find their needs well catered for in the many shopping malls, some underground and away from the often harsh reality of Canadian winters, in the proliferation of cinemas, museums, theatres, ballet theatres and other cultural facilities for which all major centres more than adequately cater.

And should one encounter the unfortunate possibility of disablement in later years, light at the end of the tunnel comes in the exemplary facilities Canada provides for its less able-bodied citizens. A 'user-friendly' country in so many ways, Canada takes great care to ensure that quality of life is high for all; facilities for wheelchairs for instance are fully considered in every planner's blueprint for new and refurbished buildings, walkways and shopping precincts.

Further information regarding facilities for the disabled are available from:

The Canadian Paraplegic Association,
520 Sutherland Drive, Toronto, Ontario, Canada, M4G 3U9. 416 422 5640

Similar information from within the UK can be obtained by contacting:

Tripscope,
63 Esmond Road, London, W4 1JE. 081 994 9294

TV, Radio, Media

Despite the call of the great outdoors, it is a fact of life that many

Canadians spend a large proportion of their leisure hours in front of the TV screen, enjoying a can or two of some local brew.

Television, cable television, video facilities, radio, newspapers, magazines and books, all cater more than adequately for the citizen who might seek refuge from often harsh climatic conditions in the world outside.

TV

Eight main commercial television networks operate, national services provided by CBC and CTV. Regional networks include ASN (Atlantic Satellite Network), Global, Radio Canada (CBC French) and TVA (Quebec).

Two nationwide services (one broadcast in French; the other in English) are operated by the Canadian Broadcasting Company (CBC), an organisation operating on much the same lines as our BBC.

A third company CTV operates alongside CBC. Various regional and provincial networks, independent companies and programmes broadcast from the United States supplement the huge choice of programmes already available. Cable television is extremely popular and Canadians have the highest cable TV service in the world, with around 62% of homes served.

Recently CBC has faced a massive slump in popularity ratings, to a point that almost threatens its existence, or so the major factions of the popular press report. Budget cuts are allegedly to blame for problems facing the government owned network, and might also lie behind the fact that more and more households are subscribing to cable television services, thereby providing access to programmes from all three American networks.

In addition to programmes broadcast almost entirely in French or English, almost all major centres provide multilingual or minority ethnic television facilities.

Television addicts will discover their heaven in the province of Quebec which with 9 TV stations offers a superb range of programmes to a totally devoted audience of viewers. Ironically it is the sheer adoration of Quebec's viewers that threatens their province's much-envied television service. A danger of too much competition amongst advertising sponsors is threatening the existence of many of the smaller stations, endangering many hundreds of jobs.

Videos – a Note

In Canada, the NTSC-system of television broadcasting applies. This system, composed on 525 lines, is not compatible with the systems used in Europe and many other countries in which images usually comprise 625 lines. Sadly then, those with their own personally recorded range of British video tapes (if not recorded on NTSC system), will find they can not be played using Canadian video recorders or television sets.

Radio

CBC controls national radio networks, providing broadcasts in French and English. Hundreds of small private stations operate alongside, some of them entirely dedicated to plays, news, pop music or whatever takes their broadcasters' fancy.

Of over 800 radio stations, many operate on a purely local level, many of them connected to the national publicly owned company Canadian Broadcasting Corporation (CBC). CBC broadcasts in English and French.

Newspapers

Canada has no recognised national newspapers, although the 'Toronto Globe and Mail' is distributed on a national basis. Even this publication though, has an average circulation of just over 300,000.

Most daily, weekly and monthly publications are printed on a provincial basis, and a wide selection of news stores sell major American, British and French newspapers, magazines and periodicals. Over one hundred daily newspapers are published, the highest regional level being that of Ontario which has 44 daily newspapers. British Columbia prints 18 daily newspapers, Quebec a lower but still respectable 11 publications.

The average regional daily newspaper manifests itself as incredibly bulky compared to its British counterpart; the padding though isn't so much due to an abundance of local news and specialist features, as much as to hundreds and thousands of advertisements contained within the pages.

Of Canadian regional publications, the following list, though by no means conclusive, gives details of each province's primary newspapers.

Alberta

Edmonton Journal,
Southam Inc., POB 2421, Edmonton, Alberta, T5J 2S6.

The Calgary Herald,
206 7th Avenue, S W Calgary, Alberta.

British Columbia

Vancouver Sun,
Pacific Press Limited, 2250 Granville Street, Vancouver, British
  Columbia, V6H 3G2.

Two BC publications known to present a positive wealth of job
vacancy advertisements are **'Province'** and **'Westender'**.

Manitoba

Winnipeg Free Press,
1700 Church Avenue, Winnipeg, Manitoba, R2X 3A2.

New Brunswick

Telegraph-Journal,
NB Publishing Co. Ltd., Crown Street, POB 2350, St. John's,
  New Brunswick, E2L 3V8.

Newfoundland

Telegram,
Thomson Newspapers Co. Ltd., 400 Topsail Road, POB 5970,
  St. John's, Newfoundland, AIC 5X7.

Northern Territories

News/North,
Northern News Services Ltd., POB 2820, Yellowknife, Northern
  Territories, X1A 2RI.

Nova Scotia

Chronicle-Herald,
1650 Argyle Street, POB 610, Halifax, Nova Scotia, B3J 2T2.

Ontario

Toronto Globe and Mail,
444 Front Street West, Toronto, Ontario, M5V 2S9.

The Toronto Star,
8 King Street West, Toronto, Ontario.

Prince Edward Island

Guardian,
Thomson Newspapers Co. Ltd., 165 Prince Street, POB 760, Charlottetown, Prince Edward Island.

Quebec

Le Journal de Montreal,
Groupe Quebececor Inc., 4545 rue Frontenac, Montreal PQ H2H 2R7.

The Quebec Chronicle Telegraph,
22 rue Ste-Anne, Quebec City, Quebec, G1R 3X3.

Saskatchewan

Leader-Post,
1964 Park Street, POB 2020, Regina, Saskatchewan, S4P 3G4.

Yukon

Whitehorse Star,
2149 Second Avenue, Whitehorse, Yukon Territory Y1A 1C5.

Canada's most popular news magazine is the weekly publication 'Maclean's'. Other popular magazines, many imported from outside sources include the 'Economist', 'Time' and 'Newsweek'.

A wide selection of Canadian newspapers are available for reference in provincial government offices based in London. High Commissions and other Canadian government offices in Britain are usually able to provide access to a reasonable range of publications for public reference. Contact your nearest Canadian government office for details of facilities available. In London, the Canadian High Commission is able to provide details of Agents-General offices for respective Canadian provinces where one can also obtain details of job vacancies available.

One extremely useful publication available from travel agents in Britain and from the publishers, is 'Canada News'. Send for further details to:

Canada News,
1 Commercial Road, Eastbourne, East Sussex, BN21 3XQ. 0323 412 001

For those Britons interested in a preview of the popular Canadian press, **Canada House,** in Trafalgar Square, London, maintains a large selection of newspapers and periodicals for reference by visitors.

Those wishing to keep up-to-date with goings on in Britain will find most major British publications available in major Canadian reference libraries. At Vancouver's Public Library, situated at 750 Burrard Street, or else at the British Consulate office, one will find a particularly good assortment of good old 'British' press publications and periodicals to pander to their needs. Most British Consulates incidentally, offer reading facilities to interested visitors.

An excellent monthly publication 'Britannia' proves exceedingly popular with British Expatriates, and is available in all major centres. British newspapers 'The Times' 'Telegraph', 'Daily Express' and many Sunday papers are available in Canadian branches of W.H.Smith. Unfortunately prices will present something of a shock to the truly homesick 'Brit', who will suffer further from the drain on his financial resources in acquiring his Canadian-style British tabloid.

Post & Telephone Services

Post

Post offices are open weekdays during normal business hours and frequently on Saturday mornings.

The national postal service is provided by federal government. Canada does not boast a post office on virtually every high street as is so often the case in Britain, and in many cities postal services are provided primarily from foyers in shopping malls. Stamps are also easily available from most drug stores, hotel lobbies, airports, railway stations, bus terminals and most news stands.

Courier services and overnight express organisations proliferate throughout Canada, perhaps indicating the inefficiency and sluggishness of Canada Post, the government crown postal service. Our British service, though to most Britons seen as offering little by way of speed, efficiency or reliability, is allegedly the envy of your average Canadian.

Telegrams & Telex

Telegram (Telepost) and cablegram communications are the responsibility of CN/CP Telecommunications, addresses for local offices are provided in all public telephone directories. Telegrams are usually sent via the telephone with charges made to one's account. They can however be made in person from CN/CP offices, a separate entity from the postal services. Addresses for CN/CP offices are provided in all local telephone directories. In Newfoundland and Labrador, telegrams are forwarded via Terra Nova Tel.

Canada's telex system comprises over 50,000 units and handles over 3 million messages each year.

Telephones

Canada's telephone system bears close resemblance to that of the United States, with pay phones available on almost every street corner. Run by private enterprise, Canada's system is speedy and efficient.

To contact the operator for collect, operator-assistance or to place overseas calls, dial 'O', followed by the number you wish to contact.

Telephone numbers with '800' exchanges are our equivalent of 'free-phone'; dial '1' and then the number you wish to reach and the call is free of charge.

Most major telephone companies are privately owned but regulated by the government. Subscribers pay a set monthly rate and are not charged by the number of calls made. In fact, the majority of local calls from private telephones are free of charge, even for those calls that extend from one hour to the next, and the next ...

Most telephone numbers operate by means of touch-tone telephone systems, the type which usually are directed by answerphone through to whatever extension or service one indicates by means of numbers and letters provided on the telephone itself. Pressing number 2 might consequently transfer you from your doctor's answer machine to that office where you might arrange an appointment; number 3 might instead allow you to cancel an appointment arranged earlier. Very confusing they say for the newcomer, but something which given the fact that many such services in Britain now operate on similar lines, will soon become a way of life whichever side of the ocean we live.

Telephoning the UK

International Direct Dialling (IDD) facilities are in operation.

The IDD code from Canada to the UK is: 011 44 followed by area code and number. Note: The zero is dropped from the area code. IDD cheap rate is from 6 pm to 9 am (Canadian local time).

Those a little reluctant to use the telephone or else unsure of the procedure involved in direct dialling, should contact the international operator for assistance; the telephone number for such service is 153.

Emergency

The first few pages of all public telephone directories provide comprehensive information for the telephone user's benefit, including a full list of emergency numbers and long-distance country codes.

Useful Telephone Numbers

Directory Enquiries: 411
Emergency (Police, ambulance and fire services): 911
International Directory Enquiries and Operator Assistance: 153

Area Codes

Quebec City: 418
Nova Scotia: 902
Prince Edward Island: 902
New Brunswick: 506
Newfoundland: 709
Ottawa: 613
Manitoba: 204
Alberta: 403
Toronto: 416
Montreal: 514

Pets

The British animal lover will find Canadians similarly well-disposed towards pets, and as is the case in the former country most Canadian families add at least one pet member to their families.

Again, similarities exist in the attitude adopted by many property owners towards keeping animals in rented accommodation; sometimes it is permitted, sometimes not. To avoid the pain and frustration that might otherwise ensue if taking one's pet to Canada, check in advance that any pre-arranged accommodation does not operate a 'people-only' policy.

Canadians, being the health and hygiene conscious society they are, take great steps to keep public parks and thoroughfares clear of animal excrement. In most public parks one find 'doggy loos', to which the dog owner must direct his pet when required. Canadian laws take a very dim view of careless and inconsiderate animal owners who allow their animals to foul public places without cleaning up after them. Doggy scoops and a ready supply of bags will do the trick if no suitable lavatory facilities are available nearby.

Importation of Pets

Domesticated cats and dogs are allowed entry (without quarantine in most instances) from all countries except the United States. Rabies exists in Canada, and stringent rules apply to animals imported into the country. Your veterinary surgeon will be able to advise and arrange for necessary vaccination for your pet.

Requirements for entry are as follows:

- Pets must possess certificates issued by full-time veterinary surgeons, employed by the government of the country of origin, such certification must clearly identify the animal and verify that it has been vaccinated against rabies at least one month, and not more than one year, prior to the date of export to Canada; or

- If not accompanied by such certification, though the animal may still be admitted to Canada, a rabies vaccination will be given, and upon arrival the animal will undergo a quarantine period of at least one month at government approved premises.

Rabies vaccination on animals of three months of age and under is not recognised as adequate for the purposes of exportation.

Appropriate documentation includes an export certificate evidenced by a veterinary surgeon within 10 days of travel, along with an export licence from the Ministry of Agriculture. This licence can be obtained from:

Ministry of Agriculture,
Export Division, Hook Rise South, Tolworth, Surbiton, KT7 6NF.
081 330 8183

Of course, it's not so easy a task as just picking up your pet and travelling; there are rules and regulations regarding shipment, documentation, veterinary procedures and so on. Several firms operate by which to undertake the transportation of your pet from his or her old home direct to the new home in Canada. Your veterinary surgeon will no doubt be able to put you in contact with appropriate specialist firms. Most such firms will carry out the entire process of arranging necessary documentation, vaccinations and health inspections, boarding and shipment of your pet, usually offering a door-to-door collection and delivery service. Most pet transportation firms will provide you with a full free quotation of their services.

The cost of taking your pets with you will not prove extortionate, and indeed might present a very small price indeed when compared to the alternative of leaving an animal behind, perhaps never again to set eyes on your much-loved pet.

Actual costs depend upon facilities required, what preparations you yourself carry out, as well as the type and size of animal involved.

Further Information

Knightwood Pet Travel,
West Grimstead, Salisbury, Wilts, SP5 3RN. Tel: 0722 72407. Fax: 0722 339104
Provides a comprehensive shipping service for cats and dogs.
Animals can be collected from your home and boarded prior to shipment to Canada.

Transpet,
160 Chingford Mount Road, London, E4 9BS. Tel: 081 529 0979. Fax: 081 529 2563
Experts in worldwide pet transportation, with door-to-door service and boarding prior to shipment.

Law and Order

Compared to its neighbour the United States, Canada proves an extremely law abiding nation, with statistics revealing a level of serious crimes standing at around two-thirds lower than those of the USA.

Even in the largest cities and most densely populated parts there are very few areas in which the tourist or newcomer will be guarded against venturing.

One theory put forward for the relatively low level of crime prevailing is that of less racial disorder, and no overt segregation on grounds of race, colour or creed as is often found in many other parts of the world. This statement must be qualified to a slight extent however, since it is not unknown for Indian-White man tensions to flare up from time to time, though rarely does the problem rise above heated arguments and occasional fist fights.

Many legal rules and regulations vary between provinces, and consequently as is the case in the United States, many provinces operate a 'Dial-a-law' telephone facility by which the listener may keep him or herself informed of appropriate local laws relating to drugs, immigration, driving offences and so on.

General rules applicable to newcomers, include such as requiring proper authorisation before any form of employment may be carried out, and having insufficient funds available to provide for your stay. Possession of hard drugs is a federal rather than a provincial crime. Drug-taking and possession carries a first offence penalty of $1,000 fine or six months in prison; a second offence invites double that punishment. Importing and exporting drugs carries a penalty ranging from no less than 7 years to life imprisonment. Oddly enough, many Canadians continue to enjoy their habit despite the stiff penalties involved.

Police

Perhaps one of the most popular misconceptions of all time is that of the Canadian Police Force comprising entirely an equal number of riders and horses. That man or woman who 'always gets his man', the 'Mountie', is in fact a popular and common sight in most parts of Canada. But the Royal Canadian Mounted Police, who form the country's federal police force are not the only police service one will encounter here. Ontario and Quebec have their own provincial police force, and many municipal forces operate throughout the country. The uniforms might change from one force to the next, and from one province or territory to the next, but you'll still come to easily recognise the long arm of the law, which you will also come to discover is a well-trained, efficient and friendly body of men and women in whatever part of Canada you visit.

The Legal System – A Note

Canada's legal system is based on English common law; French civil law in Quebec. The highest court, the Supreme Court, is based in Ottawa.

A death penalty though in force, is implemented in exceptional circumstances only.

'Emergency'

The emergency telephone number for police, ambulance and fire services is 911. Emergency telephone numbers are provided at the beginning of all local telephone directories.

Religion

As a mark of the importance in which the United Church of Canada is held, the Church has recently backed claims of aboriginal people for self-government, and takes a decidedly positive stance towards Quebec's campaign for recognition as a separate entity within Canada.

Those new to Canada and wishing to obtain details of local places of worship, will find tourist offices more than happy to provide that information.

Christmas, though not assuming anywhere near the commercial fiasco that one usually encounters in the United States, nevertheless is a season of great cheer to Canada's already prosperous traders.

Public holidays are held in varying esteem in various parts of the country, albeit in all parts that term 'public' signifies that at least banks, post offices and some commercial enterprises will spend the day with their shutters firmly closed, as will pubs and other drinking establishments in many parts of Canada.

Public Holidays

Ten national public holidays are recognised. Additionally, some provinces observe other public holidays. Newfoundland in particular supplements its quota of nationally recognised holidays to a not inconsiderable extent.

Schools, government offices, liquour stores, and banks all close on national holidays. Most hotels, restaurants and the majority of retail outlets remain open for business as usual.

Nationally recognised holidays are as follows:

January 1	New Year's Day
March/April	Good Friday
March/April	Easter Monday
Monday preceding May 25	Victoria Day
July 1	Canada (Dominion) Day
First Monday in September	Labour Day
Second Monday in October	Thanksgiving Day
November 11	Remembrance Day
December 25	Christmas Day
December 26	Boxing Day (except in Quebec)

Provincial holidays are as follows:

Newfoundland only

Second Monday in March	St. Patrick's Day
Fourth Monday in April	St. George's Day
Third Monday in June	Discovery Day
Last Monday in June	Memorial Day
Second Monday in July	Orangemen's Day

Quebec only

June 24th	St. John Baptiste Day (Fete Nationale)

Yukon only

Middle Monday in August	Discovery Day

All Provinces except Quebec, Atlantic provinces and Yukon
First Monday in August   Civic Holiday/Heritage Day

Time

Time zones in so vast a country vary significantly. Canada straddles six time zones.

Daylight savings are observed from the end of April to the end of October, in all parts but Saskatchewan. Each year, on the first Sunday in April, clocks are advanced by one hour; reversal takes place on the last Sunday in October.

Moving east to west, time zones during winter months are as follows:

(all figures are based on hours minus Greenwich Mean Time)

Newfoundland Standard Time	– 3½ hours
Atlantic Standard Time	– 4 hours
Eastern Standard Time	– 5 hours
Central Standard Time	– 6 hours
Mountain Standard Time	– 7 hours
Pacific Standard Time	– 8 hours

Electrical Current

Electricity is supplied at an alternating current of 110 volts. Frequency is 60 Hz, as in the United States.

An electrical transformer and universal adaptor are required for appliances such as shavers and hair driers in Canadian electrical outlets.

Units of Measurement

Canada officially has converted to the metric system, but as is the case in Britain, the Standard Imperial system of measurement still finds favour amongst many older individuals and institutions.

Further Information

Canadian telephone directories are amongst the most efficient in the world, and a full section in all local directories is given over to essential numbers as well as those the user might find just useful to have presented in one section, thereby alleviating the need to wade through mountains of pages looking for that number of someone, something, some particular business – you know the one, we know what we want but for the life of us the name of that firm, government department, or whatever, positively refuses to spring to mind! Canadian directories therefore include all such useful and essential numbers under respective categories in much the same manner as does the extremely helpful UK 'Yellow Pages'.

Tourist Information Centres

Please refer to 'City by City, Region by Region' for details of major tourist offices, where incidentally one will find the service exemplary and the staff efficient, courteous and kind.

A Selection of Useful Addresses and Sources of Further Information

Centre for Canadian Studies,
University of Edinburgh, 21 George Street, Edinburgh,
 EH8 9LD. 031 667 1011

Regional Canadian Study Centre,
University of Leeds, Leeds, Yorkshire, LS2 9JT.

'Canada News',
Outbound Newspapers Ltd., 1 Commercial Road, Eastbourne,
 Sussex, BN21 3XQ. 0323 412001

'The Directory of Canadian Employment Agencies',
Overseas Consultants, PO Box 152, Douglas, Isle of Man.

'The Directory of Canadian Companies Overseas'.
Available from: PO Box 460, Town of Mount Royal, Quebec, Canada, H3P 3C7.

CHAPTER SIX

Setting Up Business in Canada

The Potential

Canada has long proved keen to attract potential investors and entrepreneurs to its shores. Those keen to start up in business for themselves, if accepted as suitable business candidates, will usually find their 'points' rating as independent applicants greatly inflated as a result.

Though minimum capital investment levels are not always required, most business plans range from a capital injection of $100,000 to $150,000, although requirements might differ often significantly between individual provinces.

A Business Immigration Programme aims to attract immigrant businessmen and women, whether as self-employed or intending investors in Canada.

But as for those skills in short supply from within Canada, it isn't just any business idea that will find you welcomed with open arms. Specialised business experience, senior level marketing skills, suitable business contacts in Canada, and sufficient funds to make investment worthwhile, all add to one's chances of acceptance under the Business Immigration scheme.

The applicant must show plans for either a new business proposal or one which will expand or assist an existing business. The proposal must also indicate that jobs will be created or maintained.

Investment Canada provides loan guarantees and other incentives to encourage foreign investment. Numerous incentives are on offer to those who seek to start a suitable business in Canada. No currency exchange restrictions are in operation, and no obstacles are placed on the repatriation of profits.

In British Columbia an extensive range of incentives are offered to experienced business men and women with significant funds to inject into their proposed ventures. In this province applicants no longer need produce a detailed business plan to validate their claim for entry. Under recently established schemes, new business immigrants receive two-year conditional visas, during which period British Columbia's immigration officials will concentrate their efforts on counselling immigrants and aiding them in establishing their businesses.

Ottawa proves a popular destination for many migrating British business men and women; property prices and living costs are relatively low, and Ottawa's is one of Canada's most stable and fastest-growing economies. Ottawa has the second highest per capita income in the country, another factor that features prominently in the decision of many to begin their new businesses, or relocate their British businesses too this part of Canada.

Ottawa is rich in high-tech industries. The move of such firms into the area began about 20 years ago, gathered momentum, until now around 400 high-tech firms located in the area employ around 25,000 of the workforce. Amongst the more prevalent end products are safety-related aerospace equipment, navigation and naval communications systems, and computer software and systems of almost every type.

Those entering Canada as entrepreneurial immigrants are accorded either unconditional or conditional status. Conditional status requires that the entrepreneur establishes him or herself in business within two years of permission to enter being given, at which time permanency will be granted. The business itself must be one that makes a significant contribution to the Canadian economy, primarily in terms of providing employment opportunities for at least one citizen. Unconditional status is granted where immigration officials are already satisfied that the intending migrant will establish the business he or she proposes.

Statistics released by Employment and Immigration Canada officials, reveal that in 1987, 1,889 business persons in the entrepreneurial and self-employed categories were granted permanent residence, from which over 8,000 new jobs were created and 817 million dollars a year was credited to the nation's economy.

The Business Migration Programme

That person hoping to enter Canada as an entrepreneur must comply with certain provisions as laid down in the Business Migration programme. The programme is directed towards immigrant business men and women, whether prospective investors or self-employed.

Business experience, marketing skills, contacts in Canada, and an adequate level of funds, all greatly increase the intending migrant's chances of success under this programme. Hopefuls are required to prove that their business proposals will either begin a new business, or else will maintain or expand an already established business; it must also be proved that the individual's plan will either create or maintain jobs for Canadian citizens.

Entrepreneurs are normally required to submit detailed business proposals or general business plans, which must accompany application for residence.

The Business Plan

The plan itself is designed to establish whether genuine commitment towards establishing a business in Canada actually exists, as well as providing some indication of the individual's business management potential, the latter will of course determine ultimately whether he or she will find difficulty in attracting investment from private individuals and private or public corporations.

One extremely useful publication 'How to Prepare a Business Plan' is issued by the Ontario Ministry of Industry. Amongst the advice given in this publication and factors that the intending business migrant should be able to satisfy Canadian immigration officials are included the following:

- What exactly is the purpose of the business? What product or service is involved? What market share does the business seek to attract?

- How reliable and efficient is the product or service involved? Is there sufficient demand for whatever I intend to offer?

- What are my personal and business goals, and how do they interrelate?

- Am I sufficiently qualified and skilled to establish and maintain the business I propose?

- How much capital do I require at the outset? Do I already have sufficient funds at my disposal? If not, from where do I propose obtaining the shortfall?

- Am I sufficiently committed to my plan? Can I stay the course should teething troubles arise?

Canadian immigration officials stress the importance of a plan not only to aiding one's chances of entry to Canada, but point also to the beneficial effect a well-laid out and accurate plan will have upon potential investors.

To summarise, Ontario's officials indicate that a typical plan involves:

- An executive summary – Involving very little more than the individual's belief in his or her own business proposals and determination to succeed; an indication of business objectives – short and long-term; capital requirements and expected return on capital investment. The plan at this stage might also include a detailed analysis of market potential and current competition within the marketplace.

- A detailed description of the business concerned, along with an outline of primary business operating procedures. Goals' and objectives must now be clearly indicated on a time scale covering usually the first few years of operation. The plan must indicate intending date of business establishment, special features of products or services involved, and any experience the individual might already have in the business concerned.

  Operating procedures to which the plan might refer include such as, method of manufacture of product or provision of service; product packaging, shipment and storage requirements; sales and after-sales procedures; proposed staffing levels and estimated rates of pay; and costs of business overheads.

- Detailed information about the entrepreneur and other key personnel. Success in whatever business is concerned depends ultimately upon the efficiency, qualification and expertise of management and key members of staff. The business plan should therefore seek to convince immigration authorities and prospective investors of the strength and commitment of the entrepreneur and key personnel. An organisation chart often proves extremely helpful in indicating the responsibility of key personnel and their relationship to one another within the hierarchy.

- A marketing plan – a full and detailed analysis of your product, its price, level and methods of promotion, distribution process, and so on. The marketing plan should also identify the market for your product or service, and give some indication of how your business compares with those of competitors.

- A financial plan – here projected profits and expenses are indicated on a month to month basis, allowing the entrepreneur and prospective lenders to identify monthly cash flow. Selling costs, costs of shipment, overheads, expenses such as insurance and advertising, all must be taken into account in providing some indication of likely net profit from the business at any point in time.

Business Format

The form a business takes is very similar to those operating in Britain. In general such distinctions normally take shape as:

- Sole Proprietorship
- Partnership – General or Limited
- Corporation

These general labels by which to describe a business format do not exist in inevitable isolation, and often one finds a combination of the above working to extremely good effect.

Whatever form of business one chooses to operate of course depends upon many varied factors, primary amongst them personal preference, followed closely by legal liabilities and responsibilities, taxation commitments, finance available, management structures and experience, and the degree of control one wishes to exert over whatever business is started.

As a very brief introduction to the above basic types of business formation, we might take into account the following:

The **Sole proprietorship**, as in Britain is the most basic form of business entity, and one in which the individual has full and undivided responsibility for the day-to-day running of his or her enterprise. As Department of Trade and Industry information prefers to describe it, the sole proprietorship is 'in essence, an extension of the legal rights and obligations of the individual owner'. That person is individually liable for all debts and obligations of the business and is entitled to all profits ensuing from it.

There is no legal requirement to register the sole proprietorship unless carried on under a name other than the individual's own. Those who intend to operate under another name, or else have the word 'company' appended to their choice of business name, must register the fact with provincial authorities. Chambers of Commerce will advise on what little formalities are involved in this respect.

A **partnership** on the other hand is a business relationship that exists between two or more persons with a view to profiting financially from the association. Canadian laws relating to partnership formalities and agreements are closely linked with those by which to regulate such relationships in Britain, and are in fact based upon the common laws of England. Almost all provinces have enacted supplementary laws relating to the formation, continuation and dissolution of partnerships.

Of main interest are the fact that all partners are agents of the partnership and of their fellow partners for the purpose of their common business interests. Partners are jointly and severally liable for all debts and obligations of the partnership incurred whilst they are members.

Income tax for partnerships is calculated as if the partnership were a separate citizen resident in Canada; the partners taking their legal responsibilities into account, are allocated a share of the responsibilities to pay tax or else to claim against any business losses incurred.

In most parts of the country, partnerships are either general or limited, each with distinct features and responsibilities for the partners concerned. The general partnership is as we have already considered, based upon the common law of England; the limited partnership is instead created under legally enacted rules and regulations as laid down by provincial legislative bodies.

The limited partnership comprises one or more general partners, who assume responsibility for the management of the business, as well as liability for debts and obligations of the partnership. In addition, one or more partners take a passive role in the business, contributing or agreeing to contribute money or other forms of capital. In most cases, liability of limited (passive) partners, is restricted to the amount personally committed to the business. Limited partners by very nature of their description as 'passive', take no active role in the management or day-to-day organisation of the business, this being the responsibility of the general partner or partners.

All forms of partnership should be registered with provincial authorities, again something with which local Chambers of Commerce and business advisory groups will be more than able to assist.

The **Corporation** is an incorporated business entity with members – shareholders – who are not usually responsible, either jointly or severally, for any debts or liabilities of the corporation exceeding any unpaid monies in respect of their own share-holding level.

Corporation laws, as is the case for those operating in Britain, are a whole section of the law unto themselves, and as such should be set up only after full and detailed discussions with specialist legal advisors and advisory bodies.

Special Note

An excellent Guide 'Doing Business in Canada' is available free upon request from British Department of Trade and Industry Offices.

Buying a Business

As for those entering business in Britain, there are two prime means by which to proceed. Quite obviously perhaps, one must make that conscious decision as to whether to purchase an already existing business, or else to acquire premises and start up entirely from scratch.

An easier decision no doubt for those already established in business in Britain, many organisations and business advisory groups are available in all parts of Canada, more than willing to provide what advice, assistance and sometimes cash the entrepreneur might find him or herself in need of.

Many already established in business in Britain, have found the transition of their entrepreneurial flair to the Canadian market an easy and relatively painless exercise.

Most real estate agents deal in business and property rental and purchase, alongside a wide-ranging group of real estate firms dealing exclusively in business transactions.

Starting a Business – A Note

Canada has not of course found itself exempt from the recession sweeping Britain and the rest of the world in the early 1990s, but it does however appear to have emerged relatively less scathed than many other countries, with lower bankruptcy levels being recorded.

Getting Help

Those readers contemplating transferral of their present business activities to Canada, or else considering establishing a new business once inside the country, will find immigration officials particularly helpful in offering advice and information, and once application for residence has been initiated, a specialist team of advisors will prove ever ready to help with what documentation must be provided to validate applications for entry on entrepreneurial or self-employed status.

Department of Trade and Industry officials in Britain, and their counterparts in Canada will also be able to offer much useful advice to intending business migrants, as will Chambers of Commerce in either country. For full details of addresses relating to these organisations and others operating in Canada, consult the many Canadian Trade Directories, Chambers of Commerce Yearbooks, and other trade, industry and business books and documentation available in all main reference libraries.

Canadian Business – Some Important Considerations

Depending upon the province, combined federal and provincial corporate taxation is around 42 per cent.

And as for most things concerning life in Canada, rules and regulations for all sectors of commerce and industry vary on a provincial basis. Here we can therefore give just a few pointers to that individual contemplating setting up business in Canada. The most useful source of information of a legal and administrative nature is likely to come from the Canadian Chamber of Commerce or the Canadian/UK Chamber of Commerce, the addresses for both of which are provided at the end of this chapter.

Legal and other forms of professional advice are essential to anyone carrying out business in Canada, and never more so than during one's early days in that country. Canadians, renowned for their hospitality towards fellow citizens and foreigners alike, offer a myriad of business services and advisory groups to which that person entering Canada for entrepreneurial or investment purposes should subscribe as soon as possible.

Many businesses must be registered with provincial authorities and some will require specific licensing by authorities before trading can commence. As always, it's business migration advisors, business advisory groups, and local Chambers of Commerce to which the individual should turn for such information.

Canadian employment law imposes stringent rules upon those carrying out commercial and industrial enterprises, the prime reason of course being that of upholding the country's impressive safety and labour relations standards that make this the envy of the industrialised world. Regulations concerning trades unions, contributions towards social security and medical funds, equal pay legislation, and so on, are rigidly enforced, and again those same bodies that will prove of invaluable assistance in establishing newcomers in business, will ensure that they stay within the boundaries of what is expected of them as employers, whether on a provincial or federal basis.

Accountancy and legal services can prove very expensive in Canada, although in general such professionals tend to save the business man or woman a great deal more than whatever fees are entailed. In general, though one might be able to 'cut corners' to a slight extent by employing such as the services of a book keeper during one's early days in primarily small business operations, the fact that one is exposed to new rules and regulations in almost all fields of business activity, make is essential that one does not skimp on the services of a legal advisor for problems and concerns for which Chambers of Commerce and business advisory groups are unable to provide assistance.

Useful Addresses

London Chamber of Commerce,
69 Cannon Street, London, EC4N 5AB. 071 248 4444

Canada/UK Chamber of Commerce,
3 Regent Street, London, SW1Y 4NZ. 071 930 7711

Canadian Chamber of Commerce,
55 Metcalfe Street No. 1160, Ottawa, Ontario, K1P 6N4.

Department of Industry,
Trade and Commerce, 235 Queen Street, Ottawa, Ontario, K1A OH5.

British branches of The Department of Trade and Industry can provide much essential information relating to trading and business in Canada. The following is a selection of major offices:

Overseas Trade Services
Department of Trade and Industry, Kingsgate House,
  66 – 74 Victoria Street, London, SW1E 6SW. 071 215 5000

North East
Standgate House, 2 Groat Market, Newcastle-upon-Tyne,
  NE1 1YN. 091 232 4722

North West
Sunley Tower, Piccadilly Plaza, Manchester, M1 4BA.
  061 236 2171

Yorkshire and Humberside
Priestley House, Park Row, Leeds, LS1 5LF. 0532 443171

East Midlands
Severns House, 20 Middle Pavement, Nottingham, NG1 7DW.
  0602 506181

West Midlands
Ladywood House, Stephenson Street, Birmingham, B2 4DT.
  021 632 4111

South East
Bridge Place, 88 – 89 Eccleston Square, London, SW1V 1PT.
  071 215 5000

South West
The Pithay, Bristol, BS1 2PB. 0272 272666

Scotland
Industry Department for Scotland, Alhambra House, 45 Waterloo
  Street, Glasgow, G2 5AT. 041 248 2855

Wales
New Crown Building, Cathays Park, Cardiff, CF1 3NQ.
  0222 823185

Northern Ireland
Industrial Development Board for Northern Ireland, IDB House,
  64 Chichester Street, Belfast, BT1 4JX. 0232 233233